Accounting and Money for Ministerial Leadership

Accounting and Money for Ministerial Leadership

Key Practical and Theological Insights

Nimi Wariboko

WIPF & STOCK · Eugene, Oregon

ACCOUNTING AND MONEY FOR MINISTERIAL LEADERSHIP
Key Practical and Theological Insights

Copyright © 2013 Nimi Wariboko. All rights reserved. Except for brief quotations in critical publications or reviews, no part of this book may be reproduced in any manner without prior written permission from the publisher. Write: Permissions, Wipf and Stock Publishers, 199 W. 8th Ave., Suite 3, Eugene, OR 97401.

Wipf & Stock
An Imprint of Wipf and Stock Publishers
199 W. 8th Ave., Suite 3
Eugene, OR 97401
www.wipfandstock.com

ISBN 13: 978-1-62564-012-3
Manufactured in the U.S.A.

All scripture quotations, unless otherwise indicated, are taken from the Holy Bible, New International Version®, NIV®. Copyright ©1973, 1978, 1984 by Biblica, Inc.™ Used by permission of Zondervan. All rights reserved worldwide.

To my cousin, Obaye Karibo who passed away in October 2012.

Contents

Acknowledgments ix
Preface xi

Introduction: Ministerial Leadership and Accounting 1

Chapter 1—Introduction to Basic Accounting 14

Chapter 2—What is a Church and Who is a Minister? 31

Chapter 3—Key Financial Statements and Indicators 39

Chapter 4—Money, Meaning, and Well-Being:
          "Defining 'Development for Real Life'" 55

Chapter 5—Budgeting and Pro-Forma Statements 66

Chapter 6—Holy Clarity: Transparency and Internal Controls 76

Chapter 7—Liabilities, Compliances, and Good Practices 86

Chapter 8—The Moral Roots of the Global Financial Industry 100

Chapter 9—Theological-Ethical Critique of Accounting 122

Chapter 10—A Relational Theology of Money 142

Bibliography 157
Subject Index 163

Acknowledgments

I would like to thank Professor Amos Yong of Regent University for reading the whole manuscript and making useful suggestions. Nancy Shoptaw served as superb copyeditor, ferreting out errors with excellence, and smoothing the flow of language. I also thank Christian Amondson, Jim Tedrick, and Diane Farley at Wipf and Stock Publishers. I gratefully acknowledge permission to reprint chapter 8 which appeared as "The Moral Roots of the Global Financial Industry," in *Public Theology for a Global Society: Essays in Honor of Max Stackhouse,* edited by Deirdre Kings Hainsworth and Scott Paeth, 51–73. (Grand Rapids: Eerdmans, 2010). Thanks to Wm. B. Eerdmans Publishers for permission to republish it here.

Preface

Accounting for Ministers who are Afraid of Numbers

"Excuse me, what did you say, 'money and ministry?'" There is always a double take when the two words are mentioned in a church or seminary. Many pastors or theologians think that the communal/spiritual ethos of the kingdom of God should not be mingled with the individualistic ethos of the market. They identify money and ministry as belonging to two mutually exclusive, separate spheres that are operating according to different principles. This thinking is faulty and anachronistic. The separate-sphere assumption conceals the deep connections between the two and also prevents seminaries from effectively training their students for ministry. More importantly, owing to this outdated assumption most pastors are often not as effective as they ought to be in church management and in providing leadership for economic justice matters in their communities.

Many do not even want to know the real financial situation of their church. My former Episcopal (Anglican) pastor once told me a story about his uncle, a parish minister. At the end of each month the uncle would ask the treasurer, how is the church doing? The treasurer would answer, "all bills paid." The uncle would turn away and not ask further questions. This went on for decades and one day it was discovered that the treasurer was not only paying the bills of the church, he was lining his pockets with whatever was left.

Maybe this is not our own story, but we have been in finance committee and board meetings where financial reports are discussed and we do not understand what others, especially the chairperson of the finance committee or the treasurer is saying. As far as we are concerned they may just as well be speaking in a foreign language. We are not full, effective

Preface

participants in meetings like this, and yet we are the leader of the church, its spiritual head and the chief executive officer.

Our discomfort seems to be compounded when we want to go beyond our church's financial reports. We are at a loss in understanding the monetary systems of the modern economy. We have been given a lot of talks and theologies of money, but they have all been focused on stewardship of personal money, on how to spend our meager financial resources to further the kingdom of God. Not that this is bad, but we wish to understand the workings of the modern monetary system.

You may have searched for books that would offer a theological study of the nature and role of money in contemporary societies. You may have looked for some wisdom on the peculiar dialectics of the monetary structures and forces that frame existence and actively confront persons, peoples, classes, gender, races, and economies in a fallen world. You needed a book that would shine a bright theological-ethical light on the motion of money in both national and global spheres so as to highlight the serious ethical issues that pertain to the production, circulation, control, and use of money in the structures and organizations of economic life.

You do not detest the modern monetary system. You only want a book that will help you reflect on how to nudge the structure and organization of monetary life toward creating and maintaining an embracing economic community that brings *unity-in-difference* into perpetual play and also fosters more ethical relationality without stifling its creativity and galvanizing force. If there is such a book, you want it to also cover the knowledge gap that seems to yawn at you in your finance and board meetings. For you have long noticed that the knowledge gaps relating to accounting and the monetary system affect your ability to lead your church to accomplish its mission in today's highly monetized and financialized economy that speaks in peculiar tongues.

This book that you hold in your hands is designed to bring you up to speed in the language of accounting and money in contemporary American society. This book will give seminary students and pastors practical resources for effective (not hands-on) management of church finances. Among others, it will offer training on basic accounting and budgeting, reading of financial reports, and elementary tax and legal issues in order to develop pastors'/students' core competency in stewardship leadership.

Preface

After going through this book, most students and pastors should be able to read, exegete, and make sense of the financial reports that will be given to them by church accountants (treasurers, finance committees).

Specifically, this book is designed to provide seminary students and pastors with the necessary understanding of the place and function of money in ministry and church administration. Second, students and pastors will be able to interpret basic financial reports to enable them to contribute meaningfully to discussions on the financial administration of their congregation. Third, they will be able to *interpret* the economic signs of their parishes, effectively *communicate* them, *lead* or assist in organizing efforts to correct wrong signs or trends, and *embody* the ideals necessary for ethical/prudential management of their parishes' financial resources.

Fourth, the book will help seminary students and pastors with no training in accounting to expand their core management competency and church leadership skills to include basic issues of finance and accounting. It will also provide pastors/ministers with financial management orientation to become better leaders/managers of their churches and organizations. In addition to the accounting and theological threads that run throughout the chapters of the book there is a managerial thread (chief executive officer, pastors are CEOs of their organizations).

The methodology of the book is to first teach each accounting topic on its terms and later open it up for theological and ministerial leadership reflections. All of the reflections and discourses are designed to enable students to get some theological perspective on money and monetary systems and their roles in the modern economy. Information and ideas in each chapter are presented in such a way that the reader does not only gain training in the technical matters of accounting and money (economics), but also in theological-ethical understanding of social issues relating to the disciplinary fields and practices of accounting and monetary economics. Every chapter will have a discussion of an idea or practice, showing that the intersection of accounting/money with lived social life is important for theological-ethical reflection. Unlike some of the leading books on accounting and money for pastors, which put the technical knowledge of finance and theology of money in separate silos, this book integrates them from the beginning. The theological reflections ("theology in motion") offered in each chapter flow from the discussions of the chapter and are integral to the whole conception of ministerial leadership in the age of finance.

Preface

Indeed, this book combines accounting and theology of money in a way that no other book in the market does. This work is not necessarily one of critique but of presenting and understanding the "Spirit and letter" of accounting and money. So in all the sections, genuine empathic understanding of the subject matter precedes the critique. This approach draws from my uncommon experience and expertise.

I have brought my expertise as a seminary professor who has written a book and essays on theology of money, as a former business school professor who has taught accounting and finance courses and has published books in these areas (my first book on accounting came out in 1993), as an ex-investment banker on Wall Street, and as a pastor of a major church in Brooklyn, New York for nearly ten years to elucidate the subject matter. The goal is to make accounting and theological dimensions of money and the monetary system simple, approachable, and digestible for students and pastors who have no formal training in accounting and economics of money.

In addition, as a professor in a seminary I had the opportunity to classroom-test the manuscript in my course on "Money and Ministry." I decided to write a book for students to use for the course because of the inadequacies of existing textbooks in the market. This book combines accounting, financial management, and theology of money in a way that no other book in the market does. Actually, there are only two or three good books in this area and they do a poor job of embedding the discussions and analyses of accounting and financial issues within a consistent, systematic theological framework. In addition, none of them provides a sound sociological understanding of money to underpin the accounting and theological dimensions of financial management of churches and ministries. But this book does with its notion of money as a social relation.

Overview of Chapters

This book begins with an "Introduction," a discussion of accounting as an integral dimension of ministerial leadership. Today, an understanding of the basic concepts and tools of accounting is essential to function as a competent pastor, who is the chief executive officer of her church. The introduction provides the pastor with basic knowledge and perspective on business management, financial administration, and the accounting profession; the kind of knowledge required to increase her chances of making decisions

Preface

that will strengthen the financial health of her church and improve her overall stewardship of the resources committed into her hands.

The chapter ends with a discussion on the intersection of accounting/money with lived social life. It argues that the boundaries of the monetary issues that confront a pastor do not end at the front of the church, but extends to the larger society. Thus, the minister who wants to properly grasp the financial well-being of her church and congregation should lift up her gaze to see how the monetary policies of her country influence the financial health of her congregants and affect the productive and reproductive work in her community. Theology of money and accounting is not only about the church, but also about the whole society. This tone of our study is set right from this opening section with a discussion of the "rituals" of the making of monetary policy in the United States.

Chapter 1 introduces the reader to the basic terms and ideas of accounting: the basic accounting equation of *asset = liability* and the key principles of accounting. It also provides clear and simple definitions of key accounting terms. In addition, it introduces the reader to the neoclassical economic definition of money, which is the unit of measurement and recordkeeping in accounting. The integrated theological part of the chapter ("theology in motion") hints at a different definition of money and also points to the connection between the operation of monetary systems and the vexing issue of environmental pollution. In this way, the key definitions and principles of accounting and money are immediately situated within larger theological-ethical discourses that have always been in the ambience of ministerial leadership and social justice in the United States.

Who is a minister? What is a church? Chapter 2 answers these questions within the interpretative framework of the Internal Revenue Service. The IRS is not particularly concerned with religious beliefs and practices of a church, but for the purposes of its work it has defined church and minister in its own way. It is crucial that the pastor understands the definitions as they will structure not only her church's relations with the government, but also with accountants and financial institutions.

In the "theology in motion" section of this chapter, I provide philosophical-theological analysis of the IRS definitions of minister and church. The overall effect of these definitions on a minister's leadership style will depend on her stance on how church and money (monetary system) should be related. To help the minister evaluate her position, I retrieved and pressed into service Richard Niebuhr's five models of "Christ and Culture"

xv

Preface

to describe models of church and money. So we have (1) church against money, (2) Church with money, (3) church above money, (4) church and money in paradox, and (5) church the transformer of monetary culture.

Chapter 3 discusses the key financial reports and indicators of the financial health of a church. Here we learn about the importance of generally accepted accounting principles (GAAP) in framing the accounting milieu of churches. GAAP is what defines what is right, good, and fitting in all financial statements and in the church's accounting-data relationship with the society. In the accounting world, to a large extent, GAAP sets the moral agenda and ethical issues. While the pastor is learning to use accounting as a tool of her ministry, it is necessary that she does not limit her focus to the mastery of the techniques of accounting and money, but should widen it to grasp the whole of meaning of money in human existence. How will this be? What paradigmatic framework should guide her search for meaning?

In chapter 4, we begin to grapple with how to understand the meaning of money within the global meaning of personhood, being-in-communion (theological anthropology). Specifically, this chapter attempts to forge an understanding of the meaning and role of money in contemporary American society in terms of enabling persons to become both the agents and beneficiaries of their flourishment.

Chapter 5 treats issues relating to the preparation of a church budget. The chapter provides a simple discussion of the budgeting process and the various techniques used by accountants. The goal is to enable the pastor to understand the work done by the treasurer or the finance committee and to engage with the budget process theologically. The chapter sets the discussion of budget—the fulcrum of the management of the finance of a church—within the larger framework of the vision of the parish and the mission of Christ and also within a theological-ethical understanding of the workings of monetary systems of the United States. Thus the discussion quickly moves into how pastors should go beyond any theology of money that is restricted to stewardship, and begin to understand money as a *flow*, the production, circulation, and control of money, which actually determine who gets what quantity, when, and how. The notion of money as a flow is very useful in teaching us to comprehend how a country's monetary system impacts the economic well-being of its citizens and also impinges on the meaning-making framework of its citizens.

For many pastors the time of budget announcement in the fall is the only time they talk about money in the pulpit and seriously consider

Preface

procedures relating to handling financial information of the church with the whole congregation. But the management of the financial information of a church should be a year-round affair, with utmost care given to accuracy and transparency. A one-time release of budget information followed by appeal for pledges is no longer considered as the proper procedure for handling the financial information of a church in this day and age.

Chapter 6 discusses the proper procedures for a pastor to handle the financial information of her church. It highlights the importance of transparency and clarity in the management of church finances. It then shows the pastor how to institute rigorous and comprehensive internal control systems to effectively record and efficiently manage transactions, safeguard the assets of the church, prevent frauds and financial irregularities, make fraud detection easier, and protect the reputation of ministers against unfounded accusations of financial impropriety. For theological reflection, this chapter attempts to develop a pastoral philosophy of internal control within the rubric of philosopher Alasdair MacIntyre's notions of *goods internal* and *goods external*.

The principles of internal control are about stewardship of resources, about what an organization does with them, and what management and staff are to *become* (honest or fraudulent). It is about preserving and promoting the practices of excellence that serve the *goods internal* of the organization and its form of activity. The internal goods are those that can be realized only by participating in the virtue-dependent form of processes and procedures as well as judged by the standards of GAAP, organizational goals, and pastoral excellence. When internal goods are realized they belong to the whole community, further improving its practices of excellence. The improvement of excellence in all departments of the church brings with it certain benefits, among which are safeguards against legal and financial liabilities.

Chapter 7 begins with a simple overview of the potential legal and financial liabilities that a church faces due to commissions or omissions of its pastors, trustees, and staff. The goal of the discussions in this chapter is to raise the awareness of clergy so they would seek advice from lawyers, accountants, and qualified members of their churches and also to communicate better with such professionals. The discourse of this chapter is set within the context of compliance with GAAP, tax laws, and governmental rules and regulations that guide the operation of churches in the United States.

Preface

The middle part of chapter 7 provides a comparative analysis of compliance in the secular world of legal and financial liabilities and in the religious sphere. This will help the pastor not to see compliance as a burden, but as a way of life crucial for ministerial leadership. Compliance points to the need for scrupulous observance of accounting-tax-managerial "ritual" practices in the leadership of the church. Compliance is an expression of her commitment to the sacred oath of safeguarding the assets and liabilities of the church and ordering relationship between the world of the church, its publics, and God.

This theological discussion of compliance within the dual contexts of accounting/law and religion/ethics opens a path to investigating what kind of personhood is presupposed in the discourse of accounting and money. In order to adequately understand accounting as expressed through compliance and to grasp money we must make a serious attempt to comprehend their underlying ontology of personhood. And to craft a theology of money, we must either side with the accounting-and-market-based ontology of personhood (*homo economicus*) or develop an alternative vision. The chapter ends with a discussion of a form of theological anthropology (relational personhood) as a premise for fashioning a theology of money in chapter 10, which is the last chapter of this book. It begins a search for theological ideas that can undergird (inform, reshape) the operation of economic and monetary systems. But before we reach there as the culmination of our study of accounting and money, we need to do some *bush clearing* so that the light of analysis in chapter 10 will shine brighter and its persuasive power enhanced.

First, in chapter 8, we will show that theological ideas have for centuries undergirded the operations of the global monetary and financial systems. This historical perspective is necessary to show that subjecting economic systems to theological critique and crafting theological-ethical principles to inform their operations is not the invention of this study. This writer is only following a tradition well worth preserving.

In chapter 9, I offer an elaborate theological critique of accounting, the fundamental accounting equation of *asset = liability*. The critique is designed to do two things. First, it will deepen the student's understanding of the fundamental accounting equation. Second, the subtle analyses of chapter 9 will show that accounting carries a heavy theological-philosophical freight. The equation is not merely a mathematical expression but a neat and discerning summation of a worldview, a perspective of human relations that does not always fit with the biblical view of human sociality. The moral orientation implicit in the accounting equation cannot serve as an effective guide for a theology of money and monetary policy aimed at creating or undergirding an inclusive and embracing economic community.

In chapter 10 we will lay out the kind of monetary policy that can create and maintain an embracing economic community. In this chapter, we will highlight mutuality as the key category for understanding the nature of money, work, and monetary policy. The accent of mutuality is on comprehensive inclusiveness; that is, to include all groups, classes, sectors, and regions to participate fully in the economy so as to create flourishing lives for themselves. The significance of monetary policy is nurturing, fostering the social practices of money to fragmentarily approximate the mutuality of the triune Godhead. An ethical monetary policy, as we will demonstrate in this book, is about the continuous proper ordering and balancing of economic powers (potentialities) in community or communities to sustain harmonious relationships, reduce injustice, and acknowledge the worth of all persons. The ultimate meaning of monetary policy is its capacity to point to the trinitarian communion even as it helps to create a vibrant embracing economic community.

In the introduction and all ten chapters, technical issues of accounting are intertwined with theological-ethical issues of money. Both within the core of the technical accounting discourses and in the heart of "theology in motion," each chapter examines the thickly social and relational nature of money.[1] Each discussion is designed to provide students and pastors with the language and *understanding* to intervene in issues pertaining to economic injustice that are rooted in national and global monetary systems. Such know-how enables students and pastors to relate to the injustices of the monetary system at the affective and imaginative registers. This understanding will enable them to embody the social-justice teaching of their churches.

The various discussions of the theological aspects of money and accounting are designed not to distract the pastor/student from acquiring competence in the management of church finances. In the same vein, the provision of technical accounting and economic knowledges is also fashioned so as not to distract them from the social and theological context

---

1. The "theology of motion" section is not in chapters 4, 8, 9, and 10, which are more theological in orientation than technical accounting. To include it in these four chapters would be repetitive of the theological discourses that are already contained in them.

Preface

of the church or ministerial leadership. The two perspectives or strands of knowledge are well integrated to provide a vision—not a di-vision—of ministerial leadership. The combination of technical accounting knowledge and theological interpretation as provided in this book provides pastors and seminary students with the necessary understanding of the place and function of money in the ministry and in the wider economies in which they live, move, and hope to develop and strengthen their pastoral commitments to social justice. They will be able to interpret the economic signs of their parishes, effectively communicate them, lead in organizing others to resist injustices in the monetary systems, and embody the ideals necessary for a more just and egalitarian local-global economy. There is plenty in this book pertaining to accounting, money, and ethics to animate ministerial leadership and theological reflection for all those working toward creating a flourishing, inclusive, and embracing community in the United States.

Introduction

Ministerial Leadership and Accounting

Parallax and Paradox

THERE IS A TENDENCY to separately view accounting statements or money from the non-theological (merely economic and accounting) perspective and from the theological (God's kingdom) point of observation. This split is the parallax. Often this attitude toward money and accounting is characterized by a paradox. On the one hand, existing economic and financial terms are integrated into the theological discourse through translation, while on the other a strict boundary between theology (pastoral concern) and economic rationality and reason (profit/efficiency concern) is drawn through demonization of money and business. For instance, redemption is an economic term that is translated into religious discourse, but when a business strives to redeem its investment in a very calculated and purposeful manner it might draw the ire of pastors and theologians. There is always parallax and paradox when theologians and pastors talk about money or business.

This book aims to reach a space of discourse and practical guidance that transcends the dual issue of parallax and paradox in order to engage the pastor in a comparative, creative sociolinguistic process of translation. In this regard, its purpose is to show how pastors can appropriate accounting and monetary language on the basis of their own theological ideas. In this way, the power of accounting and economic terms and ideas to derail and possibly control pastors' leadership ethos is limited.

Accounting is Integral to Ministerial Leadership

In order to lead a church effectively, today's pastor needs some training in basic accounting to equip her with the basic understanding required to appreciate church accounting. She needs to also know how to understand her ministry as an ongoing financial activity. The pastor is not only saddled with the spiritual needs of the congregation, but she must also oversee the legal and financial administrations of the church.[1] *The buck stops at her desk!*

Now this does not mean that she must become a specialist in accounting and law; it means she must be conversant enough with the basics of this field to become an effective leader of her church or ministry. Such knowledge is required to increase her chances of making decisions that will strengthen the financial health of the organization, and improve her overall stewardship of the resources committed and entrusted to her hands.

Besides, she needs to understand accounting, which is the language of business, to communicate with a key constituency of her leadership world: the treasurers, accounting officers, bankers, tax experts, and investment officials who either work for the church or do business with it. Indeed, an understanding of the basic concepts and tools of accounting is essential to function as a competent pastor, who is the chief executive officer of the church.

As a leader the pastor can approach her existence as a "managerial-financial executive" at three levels of movements: *acceptance, defense,* and *transformation*.[2] The first movement is the pastor to accept her situatedness into the world of finance and accounting as a leader of an organization that receives and disburses money; and she is required to be a good steward of the resources of the church. She needs basic orientation and language to become accepted as a respected leader in the world of accountants, treasurers, and board meetings and for finding her bearing in their tradition. Being respected does not mean being a competent finance manager, but as someone who has preliminary understanding of what the specialists are reporting and recognizing the possibilities of the church accounting function. It means she has made herself a member of the church accounting community, which is part of her purview, and she is in the process of learning. Like a child learning to be accepted in a community, her mistakes are forgiven in the expectation of rectification. *Acceptance* is the basis for the other movements. At this stage the financial executive-pastor is passive, merely accepting the activity of others. The understanding of the financial situation of the church comes not from the "I" but from the "You" of the experts. The pastor accepts the situation as it is and learns to get around in this environment. Every one of her learning and interactions with the specialists is subordinated to one referent or goal, the survival of the church.

---

1   For a discussion of the effective management practices of the church, see Wimberly, *Business of the Church*.

2   I am here drawing from the work of Czech philosopher Jan Patočka (1907–1977).

Introduction: Ministerial Leadership and Accounting

The movement of acceptance as we have stated is only a preparation for later movements, phases of growth in ministerial leadership. The second movement is that of *defense* or work and struggle. The referent here is for the pastor to gain clarity of the church's situation. The pastor concerns herself with the financial situation of the church, its interconnectedness to the mission and goals of the church, and what it reveals about what the church really is.

The next movement is opposed to these two church-bound movements. She attempts to break the dominance of mere survival or flourishing of the church for the possibility of relating the generation and use of the resources of the church to the whole earth and human existence. The referent here is the "whole ecology of the church" and the need to transform it. Her financial management is no longer focused on the mere flourishing of the church, but the earth, the whole of the human world as foundation for decision. It aims to change the world in which the church and the life of its members and constituents strive. The finances of the church or ministry, its sources and patterns of expenditures are not just accepted, but they are also questioned in order to know if they are really right and good. When this happens she is in the movement of *transformation*. She has transcended from the supervision of the "private household finances" to *action*, to an engagement in the public realm. Money, accounting, and finances are seen as part of the overall social relations of her world and what her church does with them, she believes, affect the social fabric of society. Not that the financial statements her accountant prepares will change, but she begins to interpret them differently in ways that condition her participation in the public realm. To understand the financial oversight or responsibility as a third movement is to integrate it concretely not only into the ministerial leadership, but also into the inner fabric of *care of the soul* of one's society (care for justice, for truth; quest for ultimate meaning, movement toward God; life guided by an ideal).

The Seven Elements of Church as an Organization

In order for the pastor to appreciate what it really takes to transform accounting into an act of care of the soul of society, she will need to conceptualize her managerial role in ways that can create and sustain resources, and build bridges with ways by which modern organizations are conceived, perceived, and experienced. I realize that the church is a unique organization, but for the sake of learning and acquiring a new set of competence for effective management, I want us to put aside for a moment the idea that church as an organization (not necessarily as a spiritual entity) is unique and has special problems. I want to take you to the place of the common elements of all businesses or organizations. (Business is used here not in the sense of a profit-making organization, but any entity that receives and gives resources in order to realize its set goals in an effective way.) Every business has seven elements. To change the business or its management style is to change the way we view these elements (severally or jointly) and configure and reconfigure them. The seven elements of church are:

Franchise Recognition

Brand name recognition in the society is the usual form of franchise recognition. Qualitative words such as integrity, holiness, justice, quality, knowledge, history, and strength are important. This recognition creates economic goodwill, which enables a church to better withstand competition and, perhaps, also earn above-average payback on invested efforts. Coca-Cola is noted for its Coke brand, consumers associate Macdonald's with hamburgers and Sony with electronics. For all these companies, there is a high name-recognition of their brands (service brands as Macdonald's will say) in the market.

Relationship Strengths

Relationship strengths comprise the membership (client/customer) base that knows the church (and its products and services) as well as the senior people running the church. This strength also refers to the relationships with suppliers and customers.

Personnel

Personnel is the labor force of the church, including the pastor, staff, and volunteers. They represent the human skills and energies of the organization. These people create the relationship base and provide the service (product) skills. A skillful, trained, and well-mannered staff force is a pillar of membership's loyalty program.

Service (Product) Strength

This is the skill-set that creates competitive niches. The strength of a product depends on technology, quality, pricing (dues and pledges), product range (sacraments, prayers, counseling, liberal or conservative theologies, daycare, short mission trips, environmental actions, deliverance, etc), research and development, and marketing (membership drive and recruitment, reputation management, social justice image).

Capital

Here we reference working capital, equity capital (net assets) and borrowing facilities necessary to run the church.

Organization

The organization includes management, management structure, and infrastructure systems that lead and support the church's activities.

Global Strength

The facilities outside the church's country or in the relevant "outside" centers of operation that would enhance product and service capabilities, and build an increasing flow of denominational membership as the "international" market expands are considered global strength. This is the kind of "international" presence that enables it to leverage its infrastructure to benefit from economies of scale and increase and diversify its revenue base. For a business corporation, geographical relationship also refers to regions and areas where the products and services are sold within or outside the country of domicile.

Of the seven we will focus only on just two for now in order to understand the dynamics of interactions of a pair: relationship strengths and products. Not that the other five are not important, but that the insights we will offer on relationship strengths and products will provide analytical framework for the others.

Accounting and Money for Ministerial Leadership

THE RELATIONSHIP-PRODUCT FORMAT OF THE FIRM

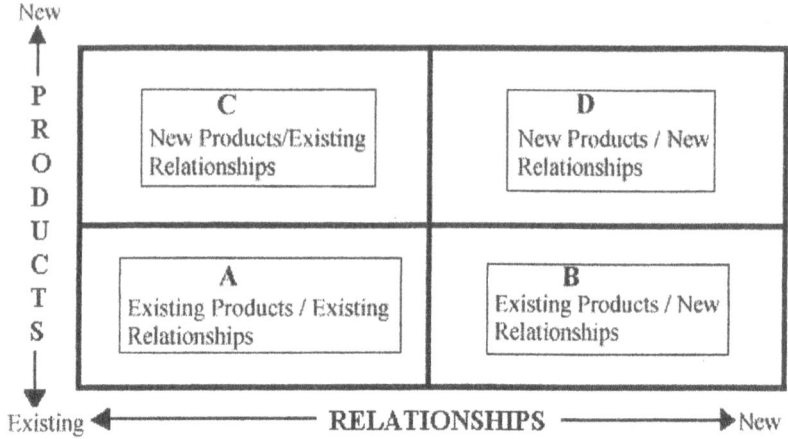

Every church starts from Box A, which has set of products (services) that it offers to an existing base of membership. When many pastors talk about change processes in churches, they think of only how to deliver current products and services reliably and efficiently. But the pastor wants to either increase membership or draw more resources from the society or both. There are three ways to do that, according to this model. If she decides to work with Box C, she will offer new services (products) to the existing members and in exchange members give more resources (time, money, commitment, satisfaction) to the church. Here the pastor goes further than her counterpart in Box A to better understand what her members need and provide the services and products that meet such needs. She can even revolutionize her organization, searching for products and services that the members might need or truly value in the future but have not yet asked for. Staying ahead of her members is the best way to ensure they do not outgrow her or the church.

Alternatively, she can offer the same old set of services and products to new members, as shown by Box B. This is what churches typically do when they want to expand. They increase their membership drive. Box D is the most difficult place in which to be. The church is both fashioning new services and products as a way to attract new members. The pastor is dealing with new membership and new products.

Accounting and Ministerial Leadership Judgment

All the knowledge we have put forward in this introduction will not be of much help if the pastor cannot "speak" the language of business, of accounting. The pastor needs at least basic training and information to enable her to interpret the church's financial statements and form a perspective on its future economic well-being. Accounting translates economic relationships between the church as an entity and its members and larger society into quantified concepts and numbers that are easy to grasp. Accounting numbers and ratios are often meaningless if they do not provide the user with a perspective and projection of the future. For accounting ratios and analyses are only needed to guide decision-making that produce future costs and benefits, not to predict the past.

Ratios are supposed to answer as well as provide numeric quantity to questions. Hence the value of a ratio depends on its ability to provide the answers to worded questions. If you don't ask the right questions you cannot develop the right ratios. If you discover that a particular ratio you are familiar with cannot properly answer a well-worded question, don't try to twist the ratio. It is just not the right ratio for the problem you are confronted with.

Accounting numbers could be descriptive and normative. Some ratios or numbers allow us to make immediate value judgment, whereas others only describe the organization we are analyzing and do not allow for immediate judgment. Ratios such as growth in equity (net assets; do not worry about it now, it is explained below) are normative. Some may think that a church that is accumulating surplus year in and year out might be doing something wrong. A church that is accumulating interest income on its bulging endowment might be seen as a good steward or as sequestering wealth instead of using it to further the mission of Christ. On the other hand, the net interest margin between its investments and its loans do not allow for immediate judgment. They merely describe the church at a given date.

The pastor also needs to note that accounting numbers or ratios are always about time and relationships. Time ratios measure changes in a particular category in the financial statement over a specific period. But relationship ratios indicate relation between any two items at a particular time. For instance, the ratio of operating expenses to revenues (offerings, tithes, and contributions). As the pastor becomes familiar and experienced with her church's financial statements, she will gain better knowledge of a church's economic well-being if she asks two sets of pertinent questions experienced analysts always ask: What is the level? What is the trend? Then she will ask what are the reasons for changes or stability in the ratios identified. With experience, she will develop a knack to identify which ratios to select and examine more closely, and avoid getting buried in the plethora of ratios.

The preceding discussions are meant to whet the appetite of the students and pastors to delve more into accounting and are not meant to turn them into accountants. In fact, this book will not turn you into an expert financial analyst or manager, but give you the basic competence which will allow you to translate the language of your treasury department and finance committee into the ordinary language you understand and thus use financial data for the spiritual and managerial guidance of the church. Do not be afraid, I will hold your hands as we take our first lesson together in the basics of accounting in the next chapter. Relax, I am not throwing you into the deep end; you will only touch the edge of the water with your toes.

A Word on Combined Theology of Accounting and Money

This book aims to provide pastors and seminary students who have no training in accounting and economics with the basic competence they need to understand financial statements and monetary issues in order to lead their organizations and lead them very well. Information and ideas in each chapter will be presented in such a way that the reader does not only gain training in technical matters of accounting and money (economics), but also garner theological-ethical understanding of social issues relating to the disciplinary fields and practices of accounting and monetary economics. Every chapter will have a discussion of an idea or practice, showing that the intersection of accounting/money with lived social life is important for theological-ethical reflection. Unlike some of the leading books on accounting and money for pastors, which put the technical knowledge of finance and theology of money in separate silos, this book integrates them from the beginning. The theological reflections offered in each chapter flow from the discussions of the chapter and are integral to the whole conception of ministerial leadership in the age of finance.

We will start this exercise with a discussion on monetary policy and the rituals that pertain to its enactment and implementation. Even a brief study of monetary policy by pastors and ethicists may serve as a mind or horizon expansion exercise pressed into the service of ministerial leadership and social justice. The issuance of money, the channeling of money as savings, the power of government and banks to create credit and financial instruments to promote productive tangible investments, and the price of money as the orchestra director of inter-temporal decisions are all at the heart of economic growth, poverty alleviation, and social justice.

The ways these factors and matters are handled in any society have a huge distributional impact on people and on the spread of the fruits of growth and development to various classes. Monetary policy should therefore not only be a target of ethical analysis but also of the study of development ethics. Any theologian that takes economic development, income distribution, and poverty seriously must bring monetary policy into the sphere of theological-ethical attention.

Theology in Motion: Rituals of Masters of Washington Monetary Temple

Monetary policy is the mobilization of a people's monetary resources for the preservation, promotion, and ordering of its work.[3] Productive and reproductive work—organization and distribution of rewards thereof—maintains the structure of mutuality of life through which a people shape their lives and cope with their day-to-day problems. Work is therefore a communal moral category, which depends for its sustenance and progress not only on the moral web of interpersonal relationships but also on capacities of persons to participate and on the right relations that are to be maintained among them. The control of the money supply in the economy

---

3. Generally central bankers have significantly pared down this definition, making monetary policy to be only decisions and actions taken to control the quantity and price of money and credit in an economy. They have basically limited themselves to using only three tools: open market operations, setting of discount rate, and bank reserve requirements, and perhaps a very weak fourth tool, moral suasion. "Using these three tools, the Federal Reserve influences the demand for, and supply of, balances that depository institutions hold at Federal Reserve Banks and in this way alters the FFR [federal fund rate]. The FFR is the interest rate at which depository institutions lend balances at the Federal Reserve to other depository institutions overnight. Changes in the FFR trigger a chain of market events that affect other short-term interest rates, foreign-exchange rates, long-term interest rates, the amount of money and credit, and ultimately, a range of economic variables, including employment, output, and prices of goods and services." Liu, "More on the US Experience," 7.

conditions which work prospers and which work weakens; and so determine "who shall benefit and who shall sacrifice."[4]

By affecting work (that is, work and how its rewards can be shared) monetary policy affects the balance of relations arising from the "mutuality of shared being" in the web of communal bonding. This directly makes monetary policy a power or instrument for justice or injustice. "Justice presses the question of concern for the whole network of relations and persons."[5] This notion of justice rejects the impersonal view of justice which limits it to rules and principles in balancing of competing interests in a detached perspective of human relations. It adopts the biblical view of justice as right relations and "the practical unfolding of concern in our relationships and activities."[6]

Monetary policy always embeds within it a vision of the moral order and a framework of moral discourse. The goal of the ethical analysis of monetary policy is to identify and expose both the philosophical foundation of that moral order and the thread that holds the framework together.

The making and implementation of monetary policy is an element of group conflict or class struggle. The struggle is not going on visibly as confrontation between bourgeoisie and proletariat, bankers and peasants, "cross of gold" and silver pitchfork, or rich and poor. It is manifesting itself especially in moral terms. The particular moral code that informs and undergirds monetary policy effectively shows on whose side monetary policymakers stand. For instance, many may have failed to notice that the significant preference of the Federal Reserve Board of the United States to fight inflation in place of unemployment has the net effect in the long run of benefiting persons and institutions whose value of financials assets is inversely related to the level of inflation. Falling levels of inflation favor lenders and holders of bonds.[7] No central banker or apologist of inflation-targeting central bank would present the matter in this obviously "crude and tactless" way as I have done. He or she would couch the argument in the language of democracy, *sound money*, rights, and battle against inflation. As Martin Wolf, an editor of the *Financial Times* of London, puts it: "The inflation tax is the most covert and obscure form of taxation. It is a

---

4. Winter, *Community and Spiritual Transformation*, 104.
5. Ibid., 45.
6. Ibid., 41.
7. Taylor, *Confidence Games*, 27–28.

breech of trust. It is inconsistent with the fundamental democratic principle that taxes should be voted in parliament."[8]

The monetary-policy struggle is both mooted and accented by "ceremonies of innocence" and the "rituals of struggle." Richard Madsen defines ceremonies of innocence as rituals that integrate a wide range of different points of view.[9] Ceremonies of innocence is able to unite people of diverse points of view because there is a wide range of possible interpretations that people attach to the acts or dramas performed in a ritual and thus not immediately see diversity in political, social, or economic interest. In America we are used to seeing the Federal Reserve Board make quarterly (periodic) announcements about fundamental interest rate changes; its chairman giving reports on the state of the economy to Congress every six months, and once in a while stepping out of his high temple to make public speeches like warning against "irrational exuberance." In these acts and speeches, most Americans see a non-politician, "neutral" technocrat making decisions about the directions of the economy and view themselves as different from the other countries where matters of money supply are politicized. The Fed's rituals is an expression of a "sharply focused sacred" free market doctrine and Americans see themselves or their representatives united on the basis of a common theme of less government. It is not obvious to them that the Fed's monetary policies are calling them to take a well-defined moral responsibility. They interpret the Fed's policies in flexible ways and react to them in ways that suit their economic and political strategies.

The biannual collective ritual of the Fed's chairman before Congress only blurs the "boundaries of their different beliefs and hopes." If this "ceremony of innocence" is not wrong, it is at best only a half-truth. Many economists have shown that the ritual of monetary policies in America is not a ritual of ceremony of innocence but a real ritual of struggles. Monetary policies "celebrate one narrow set of ideas and turn those who hold them against everyone who does not,"[10] dividing Americans into sharply composed camps, those who benefit from the inflation fighting focus of the Federal Reserve Board and those who suffer in the unemployment hangover. There are differential impacts of monetary policies on classes, races, and regions. There are the bankers who share with the government the power of money creation and hence huge profits, and those who do not.

---

8. Wolf, *Why Globalization Works*, 274.
9. Madsen, *Morality and Power*, 22.
10. Ibid., 22.

Monetary policies pit the present generation (or consumption) against the future generation (investment), the environment against capitalist production. For these economists the moral center does not hold and words of William Butler Yeats rings loud for America: "The ceremony of innocence is drowned;/The best lacks all conviction, while the worst/Are filled with passionate intensity."[11]

This notwithstanding, America, like many advanced capitalist nations attaches a sacred aura to its central bank, making it stand for the deepest shared symbol of highest hopes and aspirations of its economy.[12] The members of the Federal Reserve Board constitute a technocratic body with individual terms running as much as fourteen years; none is subject to the election cycle and takes no order from anybody.[13] It is perched at the top of the "food chain." It is charged with the sacred duty of protecting the dream of an expanding economy that serves all people as a whole and draws them into a unified intercourse as one big family. The central bank is suspended in a web of significance and meaning which economists, bankers, and politicians have spun. This web constitutes a set of moral discourse with a solid conscious consensus about what is the proper and morally right way to conduct public economic policies.

When even monetary-policymakers and bankers alike are not overtly conscious of their ethics, their decisions and predictions are premised on values and norms that shape their decisions. At the minimum, they harbor views on the determinants of economic outcomes. Contextually, and in general, Americans tend to explain economic outcomes with more emphasis on individual efforts than on luck (partly because of perceived opportunities for social mobility). Alberto Alesina et al have shown that this is not the situation in Europe where the emphasis tends to be put on luck.[14] This difference in attitude has definite ethical implications. Americans, unlike Europeans who favor some protection schemes and income redistribution,

---

11. Yeats, "Second Coming," 211, quoted in Madsen, *Morality and Power*, 166.

12. Central banking may be described as a form of civil religion—especially in the former West Germany and in the United States. For a good description of civil religion in America, see Bellah, *Beyond Belief*, 168–89.

13. There are nineteen persons on the board. The President of the United States appoints seven of them for fourteen-year non-renewable terms. The remainder is appointed by the twelve Federal Reserve banks appointed by banks subject to approval by the seven. Only five of the twelve can vote in the Open Market Committee, giving the seven appointed by the president ultimate authority.

14. Alesina et al, "Inequality and Happiness."

are willing to tolerate more income inequality and prefer focusing their gaze on equality of opportunity.

Exercises

1. Define and explain the seven elements of business.
2. Describe the importance of accounting to ministerial leadership in the twenty-first century.
3. Using the model of relationship-product for corporation, explain how your church can increase its membership.
4. What do you understand by monetary policy and what are some of the "ceremonies of innocence" deployed to increase public buy-in of actions of the Federal Reserve Board of the United States?

CHAPTER 1

Introduction to Basic Accounting

Accounting Is a Narrative

ACCOUNTING DATA OR REPORTS never come to us raw; they are mediated through narrative. All accounting is a story. It is an imagination (abstraction) with the virtues of economy, consistency, and broadband resonance. Though the language that paints this picture is always simple and restrained, it is filled with panorama and process. The accounting reports of a corporation deal with images that are at the very margins of reality. They are neither a perfect rendition of the past nor a perfect predictor of the not-yet. Yet they capture a period, a fleeting moment as the past slides into the future with the accountant's capacity to present the absent as the real. Figures and data are not unmediated undeniable realities, which can be abstracted from practices of representation and the stories they create or describe.

Accounting is a story of how an organization has worked and why it works. It shapes how the persons in the organization view the reality of the organization, how they should respond to life, and what the organization might become. Accounting presents how an organization imagines itself in terms of the flow of financial resources at its disposal and how others imagine it.

Understanding the "identity" of the organization being portrayed by accounting is crucial for a pastor defining the clarity of her organization's or mission's goals. Accounting records, reports, and analyses shape unique expectations and characters of organizations. Accounting reports are not just simple narratives of financial flows meant for board or committee meetings; they are part of the social ecology of ministerial leadership.

The accounting world, the community of practitioners, is a narrative-formed one. As narrative it also presents a particular view of the world. It is based on two philosophical ideas. First, is the idea that an organization is a unit, a single entity that can be identified in and of itself. The organization is an entity that can be succinctly distinguished from others and a set of accounts can be kept to recognize and record its activities. Second, there is the notion that equality is the fundamental principle in the organization's life: assets must exactly match liabilities (*Assets = Equities; Assets = Liabilities + Owners' Equity*). The whole process of measuring, recording, and reporting the transactions of an entity must always end up with this equality.

The social practice of accounting takes the form of ideas and principles that are clearly based on or warranted by this set of central convictions. Any effort to understand the mindset and "social ethics" of accounting as a profession or discipline in itself must recognize the critical significance of its narrative. "Every social ethic involves a narrative, whether it is concerned with the formulation of basic principles of social organization and/or concrete policy alternatives.... The form and content of a community is narrative dependent and therefore what counts as 'social ethics' is a correlative of the content of that narrative."[1] How does the narrative and ensuing social ethics of the accounting profession (community) relate to the kind of narrative that determines the life of the church as a communion?

We will engage with various dimensions of this narrative from multiple angles as we dynamically formulate a combined theology of accounting and money in every chapter of this book. This book provides students with the basic resources and skills to engage the accounting dimension of ministerial leadership; to enter into the imaginative landscape of church leadership via the portal of accounting.

The Basics of Accounting

Accounting

There are two ways to understand what accounting is. First, you consider it as a history of your church in numbers, figures, and statistics. It is snapshot of the financial status of the church. Second, it is a means of organizing and presenting key information and data of the church in financial terms. Accounting as a photograph or means of reporting on the resources of the organization works by producing financial statements, which help to evaluate the performance of the church and estimate its future prospects.

---

1. Hauerwas, *Community of Character*, 9–10.

How Does Accounting Work?

Each transaction is entered into a book or journal. Each is entered twice or has two sides to it, positive and negative. Each entry has its own mirror image. When the entry is positive it is called *debit*. The negative is called *credit*. This way of keeping each transaction as two components is called *double entry* bookkeeping. The debits and credits in the book must be equal and this is what keeps the book balanced.

Before the accountant can record transactions in the ledger or journal the organization needs to make a decision on how to *recognize* its revenues or expenses. It can account for transactions on the basis of *cash* or *accrual*. The organization either focuses on recording when resources are used or gained instead of when cash is finally paid or received for them. Churches can choose to recognize revenues or expenses when *cash* has been received or expended irrespective of the time of the service. For instance, pledges will not be recognized as cash until actual money is received even if the person making the pledge has an impeccable pledge redemption record. This is what cash accounting means. On the other hand, *accrual* accounting records revenues when earned and not when received and recognizes expenses when incurred instead of when they are actually paid off. For a church on the cash method, water bill for December 2011 will not be included in the expenses of that year if the actual payment was made in January 2012. Many churches use a modified or hybrid system that combines the features of cash and accrual accounting methods.

The principle of *consistency* requires that once a church has chosen a method it should stick to that method for the sake of comparability of reports across time. It is not a measure of good practice to change from cash to accrual in one year and in the next go back to cash accounting.

The record of revenues and expenses under each of this method of recognition has to also pass the test of *matching*. This is to say accountants try to match expenses of producing a service or product with the revenue associated with the service or product. Part of the activities of the accounting departments in any organization is to ensure that expenses are measured, recorded, and reported in such a way that identify them with their associated revenues.

Though expenses and revenues are to be matched, accountants bring different attitudes to them. The rule (the principle of *conservatism*) is that the accountant should be quick to recognize expenses and losses, but slow to recognize revenues and gains. The reason being that he or she should work to avoid the overstatement of values of assets and owners' equity.

Introduction to Basic Accounting

The conservative attitude does not mean that accountants record all insignificant events or every outlier for the sake of completeness. They make judgment about what to observe and measure with the aid of the principle or concept of *materiality*. They observe, measure, record, and report important things. The only problem is that it is difficult to draw a bright line between important things and insignificant transactions and events.

Before accounting statements are prepared and reported a decision also has to be made with regard to the *accounting period* a church wants to use for its reporting purposes. The period is usually a year and the church's financial statements must include a description of it. The description enables the reader to know for what period income or cash flows has been measured. Statements are usually twelve months apart, but a church can also choose to present quarterly statements.

Values in financial statements are at historical cost, less depreciations or repayments. Traditionally in the United States accountants will not measure, record, and report assets in the balance sheet at current market value. So when current revenues are matched with expenses, the expenses are recorded only at their historical values. In times of high rate of inflation and rapid changes in the purchasing power of a national currency, this simplification (*cost concept*) does not augur well for sound economic decision-making.

In another vein the reports of the church treat the church as a *going concern* and as such the usual financial statements will not present the liquidation value of the church. The preparers of financial statements will assume that the church will operate indefinitely as a going concern. It does not matter that some in the church think that the church is better dead, liquidated than for it to continue to be operated as a going concern.

The measurement, recording, reporting of expenses and revenues, and of all other categories in the balance sheet, income statement, and statement of cash flows are presented only in terms of money. So whatever is difficult or impossible to observe and *measure in common monetary units* does not get reported. For this reason, among many others, it is important for the pastor to know that financial statements do not present a complete picture of the church. It will not cover knowledge, skills, reputation, and faithfulness of the members that have not yielded revenues but can ensure the continued survival and flourishing of the church. As with the methodology of National Product (GNP), products and services "outside" the market system are not counted, measured, and reported in the measurement of national income. In both cases, unpaid volunteer work is not counted.

Accounting and Money for Ministerial Leadership

Financial Statements

1. Balance Sheet (Statement of Assets and Liabilities)
2. Net Assets
3. Statement of Revenue and Expenses (Income Statement)
4. Statement of Cash Flows
5. Fund Accounting
6. Auditor's or Accountant's Report
7. Footnotes

Balance Sheet (Statement of Assets and Liabilities)

The balance sheet shows you the current economic status of the church at a given date. This snapshot of the financial information of the church captures the assets, liabilities, and owners' equity (net assets). The balance sheet presents the assets and liabilities of the church at a given date. The values of assets and liabilities as recorded in the balance sheet are not the original costs; they are the original cost of assets less of depreciation (portion of the original cost included in expenses of preceding periods) or cost of liabilities less payments and extinguishments. Land is almost always reported on the balance sheet at its original cost. As you move down the balance sheet the quality of line numbers drops. This is true for assets and liabilities. Doubt about their true value increases.

Assets are resources of the church that can earn income or can yield future economic benefits. This includes buildings, vehicles, equipment, furniture, cash, prepayments, investments in bonds, securities, and stocks, claims, and so on. Assets are things or securities that the church owns which can be exchanged for cash or economic benefits in the future. Assets could be *monetary* or *non-monetary*, *current* or *fixed*, tangible and intangible assets.

Liabilities are obligations of the church, which will demand future payments or sacrifice of economic benefits. They include debts, mortgage, wages, unpaid bills, loans, and so on. Generally, those who have provided resources (cash or non-cash) to the church to whom the church has an obligation to make payments are called *creditors* or *lenders*. Liabilities could be short term (current) or long-term.

Net Assets (Equity)

Net Assets is the difference between assets and liabilities. *Net Assets = Assets – Liabilities*. This statement shows the change in the net assets of the church. It is determined by the "capital contributions" to the church (that is, donations in form of restricted and unrestricted funds) and accumulated net earnings (that is, total revenues less total expenses, accumulated surpluses and deficits).

The "earning" figure is either added or subtracted from the "unrestricted funds" in the balance sheet in a given year, depending on whether it is positive or negative. The sum of restricted and unrestricted equity or capital (as represented by net property and equipment) is the "Net Assets." In very simple terms, the net asset is the differences between the assets of the church and its liabilities (see a sample balance sheet, on page 21). It represents the net worth of the church. In the corporate world, the net assets will be referred to as "Shareholders' funds."

Balance Sheet

Financial Assets	Financial Obligations
Operating Assets	Operating Liabilities
	Book Value

Statement of Revenue and Expenses (Income Statement)

Tithes and offerings of a church are considered as its revenues. This is not all. Churches also earn interest income and dividends from their investments. They also receive donations and contributions. Some churches that have rental properties earn revenues from them. Expenses of a church include wages and salaries, utility bills, bank charges, interest expenses, insurance payments, offices supplies, and so on that help it to operate. Revenues less expenses represent the "net income" in corporate accounting language. *Revenue – Expenses = Net Income (or Net Loss)*.

Statement of Cash Flows

This statement indicates cash generated by the operating, investing, and financial activities of the church. It records the sources of cash and the their destinations during a given period. It gives you a measure of the *liquidity* of the church.

We stated earlier that accounting works with an equation, *Assets = Equities (owners' equity + liabilities)*. The balance sheet (statement of financial position) is where this is amply demonstrated. The income statement explains changes in owners' equity (or net asset) by showing movements in revenues and expenses. The statement of cash flows explains the changes in the cash and cash equivalents in the balance sheet in a given period of time.

Fund Accounting

This statement shows the sources of fund of the church and how it was used to achieve its goals and objectives. Usually a separate chart of accounts is maintained for each of the funds of the church. The report is designed not to show the profitability of the church, but to highlight accountability.

Auditor's or Accountant's Report

It is often surprising how many people ignore the Accountant's Report. It should be the first thing to check, to see how well the church has followed generally accepted accounting principles (GAAP) in preparing the report. The auditor's opinion, if there is one, should also be read whether it is clean or otherwise. The auditor's opinion does not assure that the numbers in the Annual Report are 100 percent correct, but at least it is comforting to know that somebody has taken a look at them before you and there are no material errors.

Footnotes

The footnotes are very important. Accountants often tuck away important information in the fine print in the footnotes. Read everything. To be able to give a reasonable verdict on the quality of a church's financial statements and indeed its economic health, you have to comb the footnotes.

This concludes our brisk survey of the Annual Report. But remember, this book is not aimed at making you an expert on the understanding and interpretation of financial statements. You are not an expert yet; so do not fire your church accountant or treasurer.

SAMPLE BALANCE OF ANDOVER HILL CHURCH

Andover-Newton Hill Church
Balance Sheet
May 31, 2013

	2013	2012
Assets		
Current Assets		
Cash and Cash Equivalents	$161, 586	$119, 427
Noncurrent Assets		
Property and Equipment		
Parsonage	375, 501	360, 186
Musical Instruments	33, 862	16,000
Office Equipment	28, 553	26, 444
Other Assets	15, 678	13, 650
Less Accumulated Depreciation	(28, 740)	(31,500)
Net Property and Equipment (P&E)	424,854	384,780
Total Assets	**$586,440**	**$504,207**
Liabilities and Net Assets		
Current Liabilities		
Prepaid Pledges	16, 277	10, 838
Account Payable	22, 580	15, 093
Total Current Liabilities	38, 857	25,931

Long Term Liabilities		
Mortgage and Loans	38,954	30,600
Total Liabilities	$77,811	$56,531
Equity (Capital, Net Assets)		
Unrestricted Assets	65,146	50,998
Donor Restricted	18,629	11,898
Represented by P&E	424,854	384,780
Total Equity	$508,629	$447,767
Total Liabilities and Equity	**$586,440**	**$504,207**

As you might have noticed, the numeraire or the "programming language" of accounting is all about money. It is the preferred method of recording information about a church's or corporation's activities. The structure of the flows of economic resources manifests itself to us only as dollar signs. Money is the key to the structure of existence of a corporation, and even its manifest potentials and latent possibilities. For a resource to be at all and be manifest to the reader of accounting it must be monetized.

In the world of accounting we have assets and liabilities, which are recorded in ledgers and journals. The entries in the ledgers and journals presuppose dollar values, economic worth. The values presuppose numbers (exchange ratios). Accountants see money as mere numbers. There is a whole pattern: numbers, ledgers, things. Money is a relation between things. But this is not the only way to understand money—at least for pastors and theologians who do not want to take mathematics as the model according to which we can measure relations between human beings. Thus, it is germane to take a moment to grapple with an alternative conception of money.

What is Money?

Neoclassical (mainstream) economists have a simple definition of money, in spite of their ever-raging debates about how to measure and account for fluctuations in the demand and supply of money and how to specify the appropriate quantity of money an economy needs to generate and sustain inflation-free full employment. Money is any convenient commodity (good, paper, thing, etc.) that serves the following functions: acts as a medium of exchange, a unit of account, a store of value, and a standard of deferred payment.[2] This is a very functionalist definition of money—for money is what money does. Economists consider money as anything that performs the functions of money. In this way, economists link the existence and nature of money to functions of money.

The theoretical understanding of money in modern capitalist economies is centered around the "intrinsic" commodity nature of money; that is, money as representing only exchange ratios, as a neutral veil, and as only a medium of exchange. In the mainstream (neoclassical) economic view, money is essentially either a natural commodity or a symbol of a natural commodity: a commodity that can be traded for all other commodities. Whether this commodity is gold, cigarette, or paper is not really the issue; whatever it is, it merely symbolizes the underlying exchange ratios between tradable commodities. It is a veil over the "real" economy, having no economic force *sui generis*. Eminent economist and Nobel laureate Paul Samuelson writes: "even in the most advanced industrial economies, if we strip exchange down to its barest essentials and peel off the obscuring layer of money, we find that trade between individuals or nations largely boils down to barter."[3]

The economists' definition of money views money as serving as universal measure of values (in its unit-of-account function) by which all qualitative differences are converted into quantitative difference, thus desiccating all social ties. Classical social thinkers like Karl Marx, Max Weber, and Georg Simmel in different ways interpreted money as "the very essence of our rationalizing modern civilization" and "a tool of rational cost-profit calculations." It is a rational instrument without much "cultural significance" (that is, without much qualitative differentiation, earmarking, personalizing, and non-homogenization), focused only on "arithmetic problems."[4] The general idea is that money and monetization, the twin battering rams of capitalism, have been very successful in transforming "products, relationships, and sometimes even emotions into an abstract

---

2. See Diulio, *Theory and Problems*, 241. See also Cowen and Kroszner, *New Monetary Economics*, 9; Mishkin, *Economics of Money*, 22–26.

3. Samuelson, *Economics*, 55.

4. Weber, *Economy and Society*, 167–93; Weber, "Religious Rejections," 323–59; Marx, "Power of Money"; Marx, *Grundrisse*; Simmel, *Philosophy of Money*, 279.

and objective numerical equivalent" all over the world.[5] Though Marx argued that the objective relations between commodities are the phantasmagoric forms of social relations between people, he still viewed money, a "god among commodities," as the radical, frightful leveler that desiccates all social ties and spaces.[6]

Against this extraordinarily narrow concept of homogenous money, some sociologists, namely Viviana Zelizer, have attempted to formulate a more substantial institutional and cultural account of money. They have vigorously put forward the notion of the diverse nature of money, asserting that monetary exchanges are thickly social, cultural, and relational. Sociologists have argued that all monetary phenomena are socially contingent. They posit that money is not a neutral, nonsocial substance and that it is influenced everywhere by culture. They have countered the mainstream neoclassical economic perspective that regards money as a given and as nothing more than a lubricant between "real" goods in order to reveal the meaningful social relations among persons or groups in monetary transactions.

For instance, Zelizer documents how people *earmark* money, place restrictions on its use to mark social boundaries, create separate spheres of exchange and regulate allocations to create differentiation of homogenous money, affirm cultural distinctions, and elaborate the social meaningfulness of money. In this way, she mounted a vigorous assault against the widespread economistic view of money as absolutely fungible, qualitatively neutral, and devoid of any use value. Her research has shown that money is "neither culturally neutral nor socially anonymous. It may well 'corrupt' values and convert social ties into numbers, but values and social relations reciprocally transmute money by investing it with meaning and social patterns."[7] In directing attention to monetary exchanges as thickly social, cultural, and relational, Zelizer argues that social ties and economic (monetary) transactions repeatedly mingle. In this vein she rejects the idea

---

5. Zelizer, *Social Meaning of Money*, 18.
6. See Marx, "Power of Money"; Marx, *Grundrisse*.
7. Zelizer, *Social Meaning of Money*, 18.

of "hostile world"[8] and that of "economics-or-nothing reductionism" in economic-sociological analyses.[9]

Overall, in the sociological investigation of money three key properties of money have emerged to frame the discourse on money. These are unit of account, monetary media, and interpersonal transactions. *Unit of account* or *money of account* is the abstract numeraire, the official currency. In the United States the money of account is the dollar. *Monetary media* relate to the medium, the objects that are used as money. The money of account can be embodied in various material forms like metal coins, paper, or credit cards. The dollar, the money of account, is embodied in a range of objects: gold and silver coins, greenbacks, credit cards, various kinds of e-money, etc. The third property (interpersonal transactions) refers to money's ability to mediate interactions between people, to "the connections among persons and groups involved in monetary transactions," and to the way they use money to differentiate one relationship from another.[10] Later in this book, I will argue that money is not only a socially contingent phenomenon, but also social relations as constitutive of money *itself*. The argument is that social relations are by no means secondary, but rather constitutive of money. Money *is* a social relation.[11] In chapters 4 and 10, we will further explore this notion of money as a social relation.

For now, let us take a moment to examine what kind of relationship our monetary system has with the environment, which is an integral part of the web of relationships that make life and human flourishing possible.

Theology in Motion 1: Money and Environmental Pollution

The foundation of the monetary system in the United States is debt. In order to create money, "high-power money," to put money into circulation the Federal Reserve Board has to buy government securities from the commercial banks, except it wants to literally print money. If the Federal Reserve

---

8. In the hostile world view, economic transactions must be insulated from social ties so that economic inefficiency does not arise or social ties are not polluted by commercial considerations. Nothing-reductionism fails to recognize how intimate and impersonal social relations transform the character and consequences of monetary transactions.

9. See Zelizer, *Purchase of Intimacy*; Zelizer, "Circuits within Capitalism," 289–322; Zelizer, "Sociology of Money," 1991–94; Zelizer, "Payments and Social Ties," 481–95; Zelizer, *Social Meaning of Money*.

10. Zelizer, "Sociology of Money," 1991–94.

11. Wariboko, *God and Money*, 97–122.

Board wants to pump $20 billion into the United States economy, it has to buy that amount of government securities from the banks (creating new bank reserves for them) and pay appropriate interest to the commercial banks or their investors. The Fed cannot just create money as the Treasury Department does with its issuance of metal coins, which is debt-and-interest free. The reader who is not familiar with modern monetary economics may rightly ask: Where do the government securities come from in the first place? The Treasury Department of the United States government sells bonds to borrow from the public in order to supplement tax revenues. The banks buy the debt instruments for their use or for their clients and the government pays periodic interest to the investors. From this you can see that the foundation of the money supply in the United States is on debt, not commodity standard. Running an efficient system for generating market-clearing interest rates and payments of interest due on debts is key for the functioning of the whole monetary system.

The interest-based monetary system is one of the contributing factors to ecological non-sustainability of economic growth. It is often rare to find theologians who recognize the crucial link between the damage to the environment and the interest rate. In the market economy, every producer who intends to stay in business has to cover, at the minimum, his or her cost of capital. Let us say that the risk-free, before-tax interest rate on bonds (only a part of the weighted average cost of capital as cost of equity is ignored in this example) is only 4 percent; it means the profit rate has to be higher than this level for private production to go on. This also means at the minimum the economy has to grow at 4 percent to yield this kind of profit irrespective of concern for the environment. Now this is where the argument hits home. If the economy of the United States is growing at 4 percent per year, it will double approximately every eighteen years. (This 4 percent rate does not include allowance for return on equity, a margin for national population growth rate, and the compounding of interest, which is boundless. And if it does, the years will be dramatically less.) Now imagine the huge impact on the environment if Europe and Japan are also growing at the same rate—yet we know the average cost of capital in these societies is more than 4 percent per annum. The monetary system and the whole mechanics of capitalist production system have this built-in power to grow and grow just to make zero return on invested capital.

Now that we have shown that growth is endemic to the system, the question that immediately suggests itself is why does this growth pose a problem to the global environment? Bob Sutcliffe and Elmar Altvater among others have identified four areas of concern or tension in economic growth and environment nexus.[12] They argue that universal (global) development at the current levels in USA/Europe/Japan is not materially possible because of the limits of the physical environment. Development as it is currently pursued is unsustainable because of the exhaustion of material resources and the harm done to the earth. Second, economic growth produces pollution and other effects (such as climatic changes and overproduction of waste) that negatively affect human welfare. Third, the use of Gross National Product (GNP) as a measure of development is deeply and methodologically flawed. Negative externalities of pollution are not reckoned in national accounts—thus overestimating national income. Another source of overestimation has to do with the measurement of GNP, which ignores depreciation and amortization of natural capital while incorporating into its calculations depreciation and amortization of "factory" capital stock (capital created by human investment). The final area of concern is distribution and equity between present and future generations and between the rich and poor. This tension is relevant not because of the usual politico-economic issue of fairness but because of the connection between equity and environmental sustainability. With the wanton destruction of the environment and the earth's patrimony the unborn are subsidizing the present generation. The other issue is between the rich and the poor. It appears that to cater to the poor, to raise the human development level of the poor, more economic growth is needed. The economic growth and development needed to do this appear unsustainable owing to negative environmental impacts inherent in such a move. So it is argued that in order to raise the human development level of the poor, the rich nations and classes (within nations) have to reduce their resource use and waste production.

Is there a way to think about money, monetary thought, and financing schemes that would curb the unavoidable tendency to grow and pollute the environment just to be in one spot of profitability? In order to situate this question in proper discursive framework, one has to examine the *fixed idée* of economics and the logic of market economy. In their separate works, both Bob Sutcliffe and Elmar Altvater have argued that an examination of obstacles to sustainable development must be properly situated within the grand thought pattern of the West.[13] The internal logic of capitalism, West-

---

12. Sutcliffe, "Development After Ecology," 328–39; Altvater, "Foundations of Life," 10–34.

13. See Sutcliffe, "Development After Ecology," 328–39; Altvater, "Foundations of

ern thought patterns, and the philosophical orientation of economics as a discipline (both neoclassical and Marxian) are a formidable set of obstacles. The whole edifice of economic thought has not seriously considered nature in its model and has discounted the real importance of natural capital. In the dynamics of accumulation, nature has to be transformed in accordance with principles required by capital, "invested with value," and its intrinsic value is often, implicitly or explicitly, denied. This economistic thinking, which is undergirded by methodological individualism and the "quantitative aggrandizement of value (profit and accumulation)," are veritable obstacles to the kind of thinking and reorientation of societal attitude germane to environmentally sustainable development.

It is at this point of the intersection between the idea of sustainable development and the sociology and production of knowledge that I want us to take a different but complementary approach to the connection between monetary policy and ecology. Perhaps, we all agree that modern economic thought has not been friends with the idea of sustainable development, but we need to go further and recognize that modern Western thought system, in its root and branch, appears antithetical to sustainable development. I will now raise some issues to stimulate our thinking and provoke debate about the laudable quest for sustainable economic development amidst the current thinking and practice of monetary policy.

Western thought, whether neoclassical economics or Marxian, has failed to grasp the ontologically proper relation of human beings to nature. The relation has been conceived largely in terms of technical control of nature (the manipulative-pragmatic orientation to nature). In this regard, the evolutionary metaphysics of history of the Marxists, who see history as human productive forces acting on nature in the successive ladders of development, is as guilty as the dominant Western philosophical thought in which we find the pervasive and oppressive differentiation of subject (humanity) and object (nature), whereby humans violently act on their exterior world with precision instruments.[14]

Second, let us also not forget that Western thought right from Thomas Hobbes's conception of order and stability in the *Leviathan*, Hegel's dialectic of "lordship and bondage," Marx's class conflicts, Rousseau's *Social*

Life," 10–34.

14. See Serequeberhan, *Hermeneutics of African Philosophy*, 71–79; Abram, *Spell of the Sensuous*, 31–32.

Contract, and to Heidegger's primordial *Polemos* has been variously concerned with how to avert violence or use it for the benefit of society.[15]

From the peculiar bent of Western Christian thought to Descartes's *Meditations*, the material reality is seen as a wholly determinate, objective, mechanical realm to be dominated and discerned by mathematical analysis. In this mindset other modes of intelligence or awareness and associative "empathy" in other cultures that have come to positively mediate human interaction with the landscape are neglected or severely downplayed.[16] The resources to use in reorienting mindsets and behavior patterns are, indeed, limited in the West.

There needs to be a rethinking of the idea of human *perception* to promote a more sensitive and nuanced approach to the earth and for the recognition of the interconnectedness of sensory modalities.[17] In general, Western thinking presents the human body as a closed mechanical entity, not an open and active form that is continuously adjusting and improvising to its environment and things in its world. The perceptual boundaries between the body as a subject and the world (nature in its fullness) as its object are not recognized as very thin and unfixed. "The body's action and engagements are never wholly determinate, since they must ceaselessly adjust themselves to a world and a terrain that is itself continually shifting."[18] The Western cultural orientation that largely denies this receptivity and creativity, inter-subjectivity and reciprocity, is not easily amenable to the mental attitude required for environmental sustainability or deep appreciation of the relevance of the environment to human welfare.

The dominant method of valuation in both the exquisite halls of multilateral development institutions and in the plebian main street appears to be utilitarian. As per this method, everything including interpersonal relationships, fauna and flora, as Altvater argues, "are castrated and reduced to calculations of their utility."[19] In this way, intrinsic worth of human and

---

15. Serequeberhan, *Hermeneutics of African Philosophy*, 75.

16. Abram, *Spell of the Sensuous*, 31–32, 36–37.

17. David Abram defines perception as an "open activity . . . dynamic blend of receptivity [reciprocity, an ongoing interchange between the body and the entities, the world, nature that surround it] and creativity by which every animate organism necessarily orients itself to the world (and orients the world around itself)." See his *Spell of the Sensuous*, 50, 52.

18. Ibid., 49.

19. Altvater, "Foundations of Life," 16.

nature is often denied and does not serve as a limitation on the commoditization of nature and human.

The overarching conclusion is that the struggle for protecting nature goes beyond the nexus of monetary policy, economic development, and environment. One must deploy strategies that address apparent antithetical relationships between nature and the Western thought system, which unfortunately has come to dominate other thought patterns. And to the extent of this domination, many parts of the South are as guilty as the North in subjugating nature to human's untrammeled domination. Indeed in order to save the environment and embark upon sustainable development we must all wage a multi-front struggle.

Part of this struggle will involve rethinking the concept of money and accounting. In this book we formulate an alternative concept of money as a social relation and specifically in chapter 9 we will offer a constructive proposal to foster a theological understanding and critique of accounting, the language of business.

Exercises

1. The net asset of Andover-Newton Church (ANC) as of May 31, 2013 is $538,629. Assuming that the net income of ANC on May 31, 2014 is $100,000 and every other number in the balance sheet remains the same, what will be the net assets (equity number) on May 31, 2014?
2. Perform the same exercise as above, but this time assume that instead of net gain there is a loss of $38,000.
3. Why is the balance sheet always balanced?
4. Define double entry bookkeeping.
5. Brain Teaser: What is liquidity ratio?

CHAPTER 2

What is a Church and Who is a Minister?

Definition of Church

CHURCH IN THE TERMINOLOGY of the United States Internal Revenue Service (IRS) encompasses churches, synagogues, and mosques. The government is not particularly concerned with the religious beliefs and practices of a church, but for the purposes of receiving tax-exempt status from the IRS it has outlined certain conditions as per *IRS News Release* 1930. Any religious organization that meets most of these fourteen criteria is considered a church:

1. A distinct legal existence
2. A recognized creed and form of worship
3. A definite and distinct ecclesiastical government
4. A formal code of doctrine and discipline
5. A distinct religious history
6. A membership not associated with any other church or denomination
7. An organization of ordained ministers
8. Ordained ministers selected after completing prescribed courses of study
9. A literature of its own on which its beliefs and doctrines are based
10. Established places of worship
11. Regular congregations
12. Regular religious services

13. Sunday schools for the religious instruction of the young
14. Schools for the preparation of its ministers

Integrated Auxiliary Organizations

In addition, the IRS recognizes certain organizations that are related to churches or convention or association of churches, but distinct from them. These class of organizations are usually affiliated with churches or associations of churches; they are internally supported, meet the criteria to be designated charitable organizations or public charity by the IRS either under Code (IRC) 501(c)(3) or IRC 509(a)(1), (2), or (3).

Organization of the Church

It is important for the new pastor to take a look at the corporate charter and by-laws of the church or ministry, which includes the following:

1. Articles of incorporation for churches that are incorporated or articles of association for those that are not incorporated. This instrument is actually what is called the charter or the organizing instrument of the church.
2. The life span of the church. Is it perpetual or finite? Usually churches are organized for perpetuity.
3. The purpose of the church. What is the church organized to do?
4. The internal governing rules of the church. This can be found in brief form in the articles of incorporation or association and fully in the by-laws of the church.
5. Whether the church has a 501(c)(3) status or not? A church can operate without this determination as a tax-exempt organization. A church can enjoy the privileges of tax exemption without determination by the IRS. In addition, the law (Treasury Reg #1.501 (c)(3)–(b)(2); IRS's Exempt Organizations Handbook #321.4 1982) allows both unincorporated and incorporated churches to be recognized for tax-exempt status. It is, however, advisable to incorporate a church in states where incorporation of churches is allowed. It is also important to seek tax-exempt certification from the IRS, as many banks, donors,

What is a Church and Who is a Minister?

and the immigration and naturalization authority now demand it as a precondition for dealing with churches.

6. According to the Internal Revenue Service's *Tax Guide for Churches and Religious Organizations*, in order to qualify for tax-exempt status an organization must meet the following requirements:
   - the organization must be organized and operated exclusively for religious, educational, scientific, or other charitable purposes
   - net earnings may not inure to the benefit of any private individual or shareholder
   - no substantial part of its activity may be attempting to influence legislation
   - the organization may not intervene in political campaign
   - the organization's purpose and activities may not be illegal or violate fundamental public policy.[1]
7. Check the registration of the name of the church with the appropriate county or city office.
8. Employer's Identification Number (EIN) is required even if the church has no employee. Please note that the possession of EIN by church is not equivalent to having a 501(c)(3) status.

Who is a Minister?

Ordinarily, we understand the minister as the person who is authorized by her denomination or church to perform religious functions on its behalf. As far as the IRS is concerned being licensed or officially recognized by an authorizing body is not enough, the person must be performing all or some of the following nine sacerdotal functions. They are the minimum job description of an ordained minister in the eyes of the tax authorities:

1. Regular conduct of religious service
2. Baptism
3. Spiritual guidance or counseling
4. Wedding ceremonies

---

1. Internal Revenue Service, *Tax Guide for Churches and Religious Organizations*, 3.

5. Funeral services
6. Administration of church affairs
7. Administration of sacraments
8. Teaching
9. Baby dedication or christening

The minister like any other employee in the United States is expected to receive compensation for performing these services. But the law treats her slightly differently. She is considered a common law employee of the church for income tax purposes; and for the sake of Social Security and Medicare taxes, and other payments she receives from the public and members of the congregation, she is considered self-employed.[2] This is why FICA taxes (federal withholding taxes on income) are (may be) deducted from the salaries of ordained ministers.

Clergy pay the Social Security and Medicare taxes at the rate of 15.3 percent because of their self-employment status. They pay both the employee and the employer shares of both taxes on their net earnings from self-employment.[3] Typical employees only pay half of this rate. For federal income tax purposes clergy are defined as employees of the church. Ministers can opt out of the self-employment category if he or she so wishes, basing her stance on conscientious religious objection and signing IRS Form 4361. If the application is granted she would no longer pay Social Security and Medicare taxes. There are possible future repercussions for dropping out of the public insurance scheme. The minister will not receive Social Security checks at retirement. In an age when most churches or denominations are not setting up adequate retirement plans for their ministers, the decision to drop out Social Security could spell hardships for the retired ministers. For this reason, most financial experts discourage ministers from dropping out of the system. The dual tax status, as burdensome as it may seem comes with certain tax advantages. As employees of churches, health insurance and retirement benefits paid to ministers by the churches are not subject to taxes.

---

2. See Awe, *Accounting*, 21. See also Internal Revenue Code, Sections 1402(c)(4) and 3121(b)(8).

3. See J. Jamieson and P. Jamieson, *Ministry and Money*, 133–34.

Qualified ministers (those performing the sacerdotal functions) are also exempt from paying taxes on their housing allowance, among others. Section 107 of the Internal Revenue Code states:

> In the case of a minister of the Gospel, gross income does not include (1) the rental value of a home furnished to him as part of his compensation; or (2) the rental allowance paid to him as part of his compensation, to the extent used by him to rent or provide a home and to the extent such allowance does not exceed the fair rental value of the home, including furnishings and appurtenances such as a garage, plus cost of utilities.

In order for a qualifying minister to enjoy this benefit the board of the church must designate a certain portion of the pastor's annual compensation as housing allowance. Without a resolution on the part of the board showing the designation the pastor cannot automatically claim this allowance as tax exempt and it will be subject to federal income tax. Many organizations pass this kind of resolution every year to take note of changes in the clergy housing allowance. Usually the allowance will include fair market value of parsonage (or fair rental value of the pastor's home), cost of utilities, repairs, insurance, real estate taxes, furnishing, Internet services, and pest control.

Though the housing allowance is non-taxable the qualified minister is still allowed to treat the interest payments on her mortgage and the property tax payments as itemized deductions, if she owns her home instead of living in the parsonage. These benefits are also available to ministers who hold administrative offices or teach in churches or integrated auxiliary organizations. For ministers who are bi-vocational, only the housing portion of their clergy job can enjoy these privileges. It is necessary to add that non-taxability of the housing allowance applies only to income taxes; housing allowances are still subject to the self-employment tax, which is 15.3 percent (for Social Security and Medicare).

Theology in Motion 2: Church and Money

The definitions of church and minister given by the IRS are not neutral. They are oriented to saving the government money even as they define the acceptable form of monetary relations between the state and a major segment of its society. The definitions also orient people, nudging them to see the church in economic terms. Church and ministers are defined with respect to the *external goods* of their existence and not to their internal goods (virtues and excellence).⁴

Let me show how the definitions are key to the structure of existence of the church in the public realm. The church is defined or limited by functions (functionalism; the functions are also defined as independent of specific community practices). If we should erase functions, we should erase the church as bodies. Functions themselves presuppose something prior to them; they presuppose external goods. Erase goods external and you erase functions. External goods themselves in turn still presuppose something else, at the very least, a plurality of transactions, measurable quantities. These have to be counted, and counting and accounting presuppose numbers, which are commensurable. Hence religious bodies are commensurable. So as you already see these definitions are ultimately based on some kind of "ontology" of numbers, and not on excellence (*à la* Aladair MacIntyre) and incommensurability.⁵ Churches, synagogues, mosques, and temples are commensurable. Is this not the whole logic of the modern monetary-exchange system?

The overall effect of these definitions and the knowledge of accounting (which unfortunately transforms the functions of the church and ministers into hard numbers) on ministerial leadership may well depend on the minister's stance on how church and money (always a dimension of society) should be related. To help the minister evaluate her position let us retrieve and press Richard Niebuhr's "Christ and Culture" models to serve our limited purposes here.⁶

1. Church against money. Total separation and antagonism. Everything about money is evil, filthy lucre. Money is the mammon working in our midst. Is it possible to separate yourself or church from the monetary system and its culture?

---

4. External goods, in contrast to internal goods, include prestige, status, honor, and power and can be achieved without excellence (that is "standards of excellence which are appropriate to, and partially definitive of," that work of the organization) in the activity in question and when achieved are always some individual's property or possession. According to Alasdair MacIntyre, "external goods are therefore characteristically objects of competition in which there must be losers as well as winners. Internal goods are indeed the outcome of competition to excel, but it is characteristic of them that their achievement is good for the whole community who participate in the community." MacIntyre, *After Virtue*, 187, 190–91.

5. I have adopted Jan Patočka's reasoning from his book, *Plato and Europe*, 99.

6. Niebuhr, *Christ and Culture*.

2. Church with money. The two are in dialectic situation. There is no contradiction between the teaching of church and the best workings and teachings of the monetary system. Tolerate and accommodate to what is noble, finest, and most valuable in the monetary system. Accumulating wealth honestly and using it for the cause of Christ and furthering the kingdom of God are regarded as the highest aspiration and fulfillment of the monetary system.

3. Church above money. The church as the body of Christ includes and transcends the wisdom of the ages, including that of the monetary system. There is no conflict between faith and the monetary system. Do not just reject or accept the monetary system, but synthesize Christ and economic culture. The church must simultaneously be in the world and beyond it. Lead people to Christ, but also encourage the best in the culture. Not all aspects of the monetary system are offensive to the Gospel and thus you can incorporate the noble aspects into the lifestyle of the church. Both Christ and economic system claim our loyalty and the tension between them could be reconciled by a synthesis. Retain some existing patterns and practices of business, but elevate them by giving them new meaning, purpose, and content to reflect the Gospel. There is both continuity and discontinuity between Christ and the monetary system.

4. Church and money in paradox. The Christian belongs to two realms (spiritual and temporal) and lives in tension of fulfilling responsibilities to both. The contrast between the two realms cannot be resolved by any synthesis. You balance your loyalty to Christ with respect for laws and to the modus operandi of the monetary system. It is interactionism rather than separation—have faith in Christ but work with knowledge and detachment in the society. This is the two-kingdom concept of church and money.

5. Church the transformer of monetary culture. This set of believers tries to convert the values and goals of the monetary culture to conform to their interpretation of the Gospel and to move the whole society toward the values of the kingdom of God. The emphasis is on transformation and conversion of monetary cultures.

Accounting and Money for Ministerial Leadership

Exercises

1. State eight of the criteria the IRS uses to ascertain whether an organization is a church.

2. What are the nine sacerdotal functions of an ordained minister in the United States?

3. What are some of the legal documents that a new pastor to a church needs to read immediately?

4. Is the total compensation of an ordained minister subject to taxes? Please support your answers with reasons, showing relevant understanding of IRS rules.

CHAPTER 3

Key Financial Statements and Indicators

ONCE YOU HAVE UNDERSTOOD the basics of accounting, you need to familiarize yourself with the financial reports of your church. In this chapter we will discuss a few of them, which will provide you with indicators on the financial situation of your church. We will start with six statements and then later learn to draw out key financial ratios from them.

1. Trial Balance
2. Bank Reconciliation
3. Summary of Cash Activity
4. Statement of Activities
5. Statement of Cash Flows
6. Statement of Financial Position.

Many accounting and tax experts who value transparency now argue that the pastor should not only provide the Statement of Activities (Statement of Revenues and Expenses), but also the Balance Sheet and the Statement of Cash Flows to her parishioners. The balance sheet will reveal the assets and liabilities of the parish. The Statement of Activities only provides information on money collected and expended and may in fact be concealing assets and liabilities. The Cash Flow Statement shows the sources and uses of cash. This statement will clearly reveal if the parish's income is coming from collections or loans, and the proportion of each. These three documents are now considered necessary to properly inform parishioners on the financial strength of the parish.

Trial Balance

In order to understand trial balance, we need to reorient ourselves with double entry bookkeeping. This means that each entry or transaction has two features in the journal entry process. Each is entered at least twice in the books as it affects two or more liabilities/owners' equity (net asset) or assets. This is done in such a way that the sum total of changes in assets as a result of all the transactions equals the changes in liabilities/owners' equity. Without this equality the books will not be balanced.

Let me give an example. The church receives a contribution of $40,000 from one of its members for its unrestricted fund. The cash account will increase by $40,000 and the unrestricted fund account will also increase by $40,000. Note that this entry affects the categories of assets (cash) and liabilities/net assets and these amounts are posted to the ledger (file of accounts).

Suppose that the church pays out $3000 as Prepaid Utilities to its heating oil company.

This is how it will look now:

Entry Number	Cash	+	Prepaid Utilities	=	Owner's Equity
(1)	$40,000				+$40,000
(2)	-3,000		+$3,000		
Balances	$37,000	+	$3,000	=	$40,000

Instead of presenting the data as we have done above with a plus or a minus sign, they can also be presented in a schema that looks like the letter T. This representation is called the *T-account*. With the T-account, additions appear on one side and subtractions on the other. Additions or positive numbers (signifying increases) appear on the left side and negative quantities (signifying decreases) go to the right side, if the account is an asset account. The reverse is the case for liabilities and owners' equity accounts. Increases (positive balances) go to the left and decreases (negative balances) to the left.

The transactions in the cash account can be represented schematically as shown below. Once again a member donated $40,000 to his church and of this amount $3000 was paid to the heating oil company.

Key Financial Statements and Indicators

Cash

(+)		(-)	
Beginning Balance	0	Payment	3,000
Receipt	40,000		
Ending Balance	$37,000		

Net Assets (Owners' Equity)

(-)	(+)	
	Beginning Balance	0
	Unrestricted Fund	40,000
	Ending Balance	$40,000

We are inching our way to the trial balance and there is one more set of terms you need to know before we reach there: *debit and credit*. Debit simply means an amount on the left side of the T-account and credit is an amount on the right side. Now depending on whether the debit is for an asset or liability, it either represents an increase or decrease. Debit (Dr.) when associated with an asset account is a positive balance, signifying an increase. But it is a decrease when it is a liability account. Credit (Cr.) is a decrease in amount under asset account, and an increase in amount under liability account. This is why when you deposit a paycheck into a bank account the bank credits your account, because it is an increase of liability to it. But you will debit your Cash account in your ledger as it is an asset account.

Assets		Liability	
(+)	(-)	(-)	(+)
Dr.	Cr.	Dr.	Cr.

The trial balance is a list of the account balances, showing all credits and debits at a given time, the date of the report. The rule is that the individual sum of the credits and debits representing specific transactions during the given period should be equal. In the trial balance, you will usually have credit balances in the assets and expense accounts and debit balances in the liability, net asset, and income accounts. When it is balanced the difference between the sum of credits and the sum of debits is equal to zero.

Exhibit 3–1
Unadjusted Trial Balance
As of December 31, 20X3

	Debit	Credit
Cash	40,000	
Furniture and Equipment	35,000	
Prepaid Utilities	5,000	
Pastor Housing Allowance	15,000	
Salaries and Wages Payable		9,000
Contributions		1,387,464.3
Interest Income		78.25
Postage	42.50	
Sunday School Supplies	1,500	
Year-to-date surplus/deficit	1,300,000	
Total	$1,396,542.5	$1,396,542.5

This first run is usually called the adjusted trial balance. For churches that are on accrual basis of accounting there are usually entries, debits, and credits, which are not due to transactions but must be captured if an accurate account is to be reported. Two of such adjusting entries will be depreciation of equipment and amortization of prepaid utilities. The most important thing to remember is that the trial balance must balance and that assets and expense accounts should have debit balances, while liability, net assets (equity), and income accounts should have credit balances.

Bank Reconciliation Statement

This statement is easy to understand. It reconciles the church's bank statement giving the amount of cash in its account with what is in the church's own checkbook record. There are four steps involved in reconciling the account.

1. State the balance as reported in the bank's statement.
2. Subtract the total of all outstanding checks.
3. Add all deposits in transit, those that have not been captured in the bank's statement.
4. The sum of Steps 1 to 3 is the adjusted bank balance and this should be equal to the figure in the church's checkbook record.

This statement is prepared each month to find out differences between the church's books and the bank statement and the reasons for them.

Summary of Cash Activity

This process is also easy to prepare or to interpret. It also involves four steps:

1. State the amount of Cash Balance as of November 30, 20x3.
2. Add to this amount all the cash that came in (usually from contributions, rent, and interest income) from December 1 to 31. This is for the month of December.
3. Deduct cash transactions relating to expenses, withdrawals, etc., from December 1 to 31.
4. The net balance is the Cash balance as of December 31, 20x3.

This final amount is the beginning balance for January 1, 20x4, just as the ending balance of November is the beginning balance of December. It is also important to note that ending cash reported on the bank reconciliation statement should match the cash balance in the Summary of Cash Activity.

It is important to pay close attention to these numbers. A decreasing trend may mean that members are giving less or that expenses are creeping up and need to be watched. But if there is an increasing trend then we have a different problem. The finance committee needs to make a decision on investing projected excess cash in secured instruments.

Accounting and Money for Ministerial Leadership

Statement of Activity (Statement of Revenue and Expenses)

EXHIBIT 3-2

Andover-Newton Hill Church
Statement of Activities
For the Year Ended December 31, 20X3

	Unrestricted	Temporarily Restricted	Permanently Restricted	Total
Contributions and other Income				
Offerings, Pledges, Program Offerings	$272,000.00			$272,000.00
Building Funds		11,467.13		11,467.13
Interest and Net Gains on Investments	500.00	30,000.00	6,213.04	36,713.04
Total Income	272,500.00	41,467.13	6,213.04	320,180.17
Expenses				
Administrative Expenses	27,717.96			27,717.96
Payroll and Benefits	150,678.00			150,678.00
Utilities and Other Expenses	4,573.20			4,573.20
Programs	77,070.10			77,070.10
Total Expenses	260,039.26			260,039.26
Increase (decrease) in net assets	12,460.74	41,467.13	6,213.04	60,140.91
Net Assets, beginning of year	406,629.00	120,000.00	12,000.00	538,629.00
Net Assets, end of year	**$419,089.74**	**$161,467.13**	**$18,213.04**	**$598,769.91**

The Statement of Activity (also known as Statement of Revenue and Expenses) is simply called the income statement in corporate parlance. It provides information on a church's revenues and support, expenses, and changes in net assets (fund balances) for a period to time, such as one month, a quarter, six months, or a year. This statement presents sources of income for the operations and activities of the church and how the resources that came in were used. It is required by Statement of Financial Accounting Standards (SFAS) Numbers 116 and 117 that the statement of activity show changes in restricted, temporary restricted, permanently restricted, and total net assets. The Financial Accounting Standards Board (FASB) is the body that issued the standards and part of the changes that came with SFAS 116 and 117 is that there are now three required financial statements: (1) Statement of Financial Position (Balance Sheet), (2) Statement of Activity, and (3) Statement of Cash Flows.

Statement of Cash Flows

The statement of cash flows provides information on the sources and uses of cash, receipts and disbursements, during a given period of time. The statement will indicate if cash receipts and disbursements were from/for operating, investing, or financing activity. Operating usage of cash flows relates to cash that comes in as contributions and offerings, and expenses will relate to money spent to operate the church. This number is usually positive. The investing cash flows reflects money spent to acquire equipments and property and it is usually negative, except when the church sold some of its assets. Simply, investment activities relate to capital acquisition and dispositions, investment and disinvestment activities. The financial cash flows reflect cash coming in as a result of church borrowings and repayments of debts.

The cash flow statement is usually divided into three segments: Operating Activities, Investing Activities, and Financing Activities.

EXHIBIT 3–3

Andover-Newton Hill Church
Statement of Cash Flows
For the Year Ended December 31, 20X3

Cash from Operating Activities	
Increase in Net Assets	$60,140.91
Adjustments to reconcile changes in net assets to cash from Operating Activities	
Depreciation	16,994.16
Decrease in prepaid assets	2,599.00
Increase in accounts payable	637.23
Decrease in accrued expenses	(6,429.78)
Net Cash provided by Operating Activities	**73,941.52**
Cash used for Investing Activities	
Purchase of Property and Equipment	(23,500)
Sale of equipment	5,000
Net Cash provided by Investing Activities	(18,500)
Cash used for Financing Activities	
Payments on loans and borrowings	(7,705)
Increase in Cash and Cash Equivalents	47,736.52
Cash and cash equivalents, beginning of year	121,586.00
Cash and cash equivalents, end of year	**$169,322.52**

Accounting and Money for Ministerial Leadership

Statement of Financial Position

We have already introduced the Statement of Financial Position in the introductory chapter. It shows the assets, liabilities, and net assets of the church at a given date. While the Statements of Activities and the Cash Flows record transactions and events over a period of time, the Statement of Financial Position (Balance Sheet) presents an overview of the church financial position at a particular date. Below is the balance sheet of Andover-Hill Church on December 31, 20x3. Please note that the "Cash and cash equivalents" in this statement matches what you have in the Statement of Cash Flows. Also net assets number is the same in the Statement of Financial Position and the Statement of Activities.

Exhibit 3–4

Andover-Newton Hill Church
Statement of Financial Position
For the Year Ended December 31, 20X3

Assets	
Cash and cash equivalents	$169,322.52
Other assets	$53,334.22
Property and equipment	443,354.00
Total Assets	$666,010.74
Liabilities	
Accounts payable	23,580.00
Accrued expenses	16,277.00
Debts	27,383.83
Total Liabilities	67,240.83
Net Assets	
Unrestricted	419,089.74
Temporarily restricted	161,467.13
Permanently restricted	18,213.04
Total Net Assets	598,769.91
Total Liabilities and Net Assets	**$666,010.74**

Risk Analysis: Key Financial Indicators

One of the ways a pastor can get a handle on the finances of her church is by learning to calculate some key indicators. Key indicators are basically ratios and they help analysts and pastors alike to evaluate the potential risks the organization faces. Risk is a very difficult and elusive concept to define. Financial analysts, investors, and accountants do not have a precise definition. Nonetheless, it is generally believed that it involves expected security returns, incomes, or payments not materializing. The expected outcome may fluctuate in value and the investor is, most importantly, vulnerable to volatility of incomes or returns. For instance, a ratio like the current assets to current liabilities, which is called *current ratio*, is a measure of liquidity. The liquidity ratio of a church indicates whether or not the church is in a good position to meet its current obligations.

The financial analyst when examining risk is interested in those events that could derail his prediction and estimation of value and cash-generating ability of the firm, church, or organization. The type and nature of risk examined depend on the purpose of the analyst or investor. For a prospective bondholder who will not share in the future growth of earnings, the risk of investment may be measured by the safety margin against default. This kind of investor or lender may examine risk in terms of the issuer's (the borrowing firm's, church's, or organization's) ability to meet obligations and the fundamental structure of the debt instruments to see if it offers protection to the bondholder. Hence the first step in analyzing risk is to determine the purpose and tenor of investment. Thereafter, examine those complex and independent variables that impact on the issuer's (the firm's, church's, organization's) capacity to generate cash flows, and its ability to create value as well as increase book value (equity). Also, the financial analyst will examine the determinants of the volatility of earnings, operating earnings, and cash flows over the life of the investment.

Now that you know how the mind of the analyst works, you can understand how your church will be evaluated when it goes before a financial institution to raise loans. The risk perspective and the relevant ratios that help the analyst to ground his understanding are also some of the tools the pastor needs to understand the financial health of her church. She needs them to evaluate from time to time the risk that her church faces or to be able to hold a reasonable conversation with the finance committee or board members when the financial well-being of the church is being discussed.

Most of the accounting data we have examined in this chapter and the ones leading up to it could be employed to obtain an indication of risk or financial strength for a church. For instance, positive cash flow from operations means that the core activities of the church are generating enough cash to cover its basic operating expenses. But if the cash flow from operations is negative over a period of years and the bulk of cash flow is coming from either financing or investment it portends a rocky future for the church. Increasing cash flow from investment means that the church is selling off its property and equipment to fund its general operations. Increasing cash flow from financing, while cash flow from operations is consistently negative, means the general operations of the church is funded through borrowing or selling off investment securities. Ratios are very useful in this regard, if you know how to generate and interpret them.

Ratios

$$\text{Debt to Asset Ratio} = \frac{\text{Total Liabilities}}{\text{Total Assets}}$$

This ratio measures what proportion of the assets of the church is paid for by loans, bonds, or borrowing. In addition, this ratio gives an indication of the ability of the church to withstand losses (such as drops in collections and contributions or losses in financial investments) without impairing the interest of its creditors.

According to the figures in Exhibit 3–4 (Statement of Financial Position) the numbers will be $67,241/666,011 = 10.09$ percent. The lower the ratio the better it is. But note that the total liabilities number does not include the net assets (equity). Technically, the net asset is a liability (money contributed to the church by its owners) and as such some analysts might include it, raising the percentage.

Key Financial Statements and Indicators

Total Debt to Net Asset (Equity) Ratio = $\dfrac{\text{Total Liabilities (Current liab. + Long Term Debt)}}{\text{Net Assets}}$

$$= \dfrac{\$67{,}241}{\$598{,}770}$$

$$= 11.22 \text{ percent}$$

This ratio helps the analyst to determine the level of non-equity capital (non-owners' contributions, investments, or funds) in the church and its long-term ability of make payments to its lenders, suppliers of capital. If the church has borrowed thousands or millions of dollars to build a new edifice, the analyst may be prompted to calculate something like the "times interest earned ratio," which is the net surplus of a given year plus depreciation divided by interest charges. The times-earned ratio is concerned with the ability of the church to generate income from its general operations to meet debt service obligations.

On the whole, ratios are often organized to tell a particular story. If you are interested in the ability of the church to meet current debt, you will be concerned with liquidity ratios.

Liquidity Ratios

Current Ratio = $\dfrac{\text{Current Assets}}{\text{Current Liabilities}}$

Current assets is cash and cash equivalent and other assets (such as marketable securities, accounts receivables, inventory) that are reasonably expected to be converted into cash within a year or operating cycle. Current liabilities are liabilities of an organization that are expected to be settled within a year. They include accounts payable, accrued expenses, income tax payable, and short-terms notes payable.

This ratio tells you if the church has enough current assets that it can convert into cash to meet liability/debt obligations in the short run. You will get a better interpretation if you examine this ratio in the light of the church's history or the denominational average.

This ratio assumes that the current asset will be used to meet current liabilities, if the need arises. Some analysts are not comfortable with this measure. They would rather get an indication of the adequacy of current assets (that is, cash and marketable securities) to meet projected daily expenditures from operations. They want to know if the church's liquid assets will be sufficient to satisfy daily operational expenses. Do not worry about this ratio (defensive ratio), unless your church is under severe financial stress.

In closing, let me state that all these ratios will not give you a total picture of the future financial viability of your church. At best they give only a perspective of risk specific to your internal operations. This is so because there is also environment-wide risk that all churches face and overall changes in the economy may expose your vulnerable flank. Your church's vulnerability will depend on the degree to which changes in its finances are correlated with changes in the overall economy.

Theology in Motion 3: Statements and Spheres of Life

The statements we have examined so far have shown that the accounting world of the church is organized into categories or spheres. Though each category has its own particular transactions and events and a specific way it is presented, they are all permeated by the same generally accepted accounting principles (GAAP), which acts as their vital, animating force. GAAP represents the power and logic of the accounting world or mindset, an expression of the essential of the current worldview of accounting profession in recordable reality. It is an expression of the philosophy and convention of the profession, which has been grasped and formulated as the practical (existential) set of ideas and thus stands in judgment of all records that organize, measure, and report an organization's information in financial terms.

Though the statements are undergirded by GAAP, each is treated (presented) differently and the accountant cannot willy-nilly transfer the "values" of one category or sphere to another without breaking the rules, ethos of the financial-accounting recording world created by GAAP. For instance, property and equipment can be depreciated and accumulated depreciation recorded in the balance sheet, but cash is never depreciated.

There is something in all these that can inform us about money and spheres of life in the wider society. The work of Princeton University economic sociologist Viviana Zelizer has shown us that even though money is fungible and easily exchangeable people treat it differently. She has put forward the notion of the diverse nature of money, asserting that monetary exchanges are thickly social, cultural, and relational. Zelizer documents how people *earmark* money, place restrictions on its use to mark social boundaries, create separate spheres of exchange and regulate allocations to create differentiation of homogenous money, affirm cultural distinctions, and elaborate the social meaningfulness of money. In this way, she mounted a vigorous assault against the widespread economistic view of money as absolutely fungible, qualitatively neutral, and devoid of any use value. Her research has shown that money is "neither culturally neutral nor socially anonymous. It may well 'corrupt' values and convert social ties into numbers, but values and social relations reciprocally transmute money by investing it with meaning and social patterns."[1]

Abraham Kuyper has also argued that there are spheres of life, each with its own values, spiritual and moral energies. The spheres of life are the institutionalized patterns that guide and house the key vital forces or energies of every society. Each of these spheres are in turn permeated by the certain ethos, force or energy it houses. For us to live an appropriately good, ethical life we must learn to navigate these spheres severally and jointly. And living a good life means, among other things, not commingling the energies. For instance, in the family sphere, eros is the controlling force, but when it is taken into the office it could be turned into a negative force for sexual harassment and nepotism. Money or exchange is the force operating in the economic sphere of life, but when its principles are brought into the family it is frowned upon. If money is exchanged between husband and wife as payment for sex then a matter of the family sphere has been inappropriately transferred into the economic realm. We call it prostitution. What is a proper and improper commingling in every society is conditioned by religion or worldview, which defines the whole value system. It is religion (worldview) that defines what is right, good, or fitting in the each of the spheres and in the society as a whole.

Theological-ethicist Max Stackhouse pays a great deal of attention to how the spiritual and moral energies condition human flourishing and civilization. He argues that no civilization exists without their viable integration. Following Kuyper he has categorized them into five powers: eros, mars, the muses, mammon, and dominion (worldview, comprehensive moral vision, religion). "Humans are sexual, political, economic, cultural, and religious creatures. Each one of these dimensions of life involves a certain potentiality and needs an institutional matrix to house, guide and

---

1. Zelizer, *Social Meaning of Money*, 18.

channel its energies."[2] They are organized into *spheres* of life. Eros relates to the family sphere, muses to the arts and mass media, mars (violence) to the political, mammon to economy, and religion to the whole society. Religion defines what is right, good, and fitting in the other spheres and in human relationship with God.

Stackhouse states that the five forms of spiritual energies invite and even capture people's loyalties[3] and these not only enable people to move beyond the boundaries and capabilities left to them by their ancestors, but also sometimes, and too often, anchor them to antiquated practices, institutions, and beliefs. These spiritual energies not only guide social practices, they are implicated in the human drive toward transcendence and the future. In an extensive exchange with this author, Stackhouse provided useful conceptual resources to help us understand the moral issues involved in the operation of these powers. It bears to quote him at length here:

> The spiritual energies all have an element of ecstasy and transcendence in them. And each has been taken as a means of salvation. The joy of sexual intercourse involves loosing oneself in response to another and the potential production of children in whom one survives beyond one's life. The creativity of the arts involves a quest for inspiration and a capacity to inspire others as well as leaving a legacy for the ages. The heroism of military valor, and possible sacrificing of oneself for a people or a nation or a political system brings that kind of honor which is remembered in statues, tales, and song. And the production or accumulation of wealth can lead to plenty that can save self, family, or society from want. And religion can be authentic or an illusory ideology accordingly as it seeks to receive and heed revelation or to construct rites and rituals to make the divine do what we want (magic).
>
> These powers are necessary for human existence and are all potentially good; but they are all also prone to idolatry—to the preoccupation, worship, or trust in them on their own terms.

---

2. Stackhouse, introduction, 2:5. In another place, he writes:
People carve out spheres of social activity, clusters of institutions that house, guide, and constrain, and in certain ways, permit, even encourage, these powers to operate. Each sphere is regulated by customary or legislated rules, and each is defined by its own specification of ends and means, as these accord with the nature of the activity and its place in the whole society or culture. Each sphere develops methods of fulfilling its own standards, ways to mark accomplished goals, definitions of excellence, and standards of success. (See Stackhouse, *God and Globalization*, 1:39.)

3. Stackhouse, introduction, 1:35.

Key Financial Statements and Indicators

Thus, these contexts of life need to be channeled and constrained by institutions that reflect what is righteous (which we study in the sub-discipline of deontology).

We can see this in each sphere: a rightly ordered eros, in a good family, makes a great contribution to the perpetuation of the species and the formation of persons of character for the future. Just as the arts, rightly disciplined, express the height and depths of human experience and reveal possibilities of what could be that are otherwise not present. And a rightly ordered use of mars and even mammon can approximate a politics and an economics that advances security and plenty. Finally, all these also need to have their potential contributions to the good guided toward the ultimate good, known only through an adequate eschatology, which transforms natural teleology.... Theologically, we can ask whether each of these righteously ordered spheres of life, each driven by a powerful spiritual energy, can contribute to that which coincides with the Kingdom of God which is working within and among us. That is the question of which dominion is good for the whole in a globalizing era.[4]

The task of developing a theology of accounting and money is to think through how religion (worldview) can help us to shape the forces of each sphere for all human flourishing and improved relationship with God. And in this vein, the key concern is how the forces that control economy and money could be viably integrated in all spheres of society without undermining the social fabric and long-run morality of such a society. Another concern is to examine the "religious" role played by GAAP in financial accounting. GAAP is what defines what is right, good, and fitting in all financial statements and in the organization's accounting-data relationship to the society. In playing this vital role, GAAP in a way sets the moral agenda and ethical issues not only of the financial accounting world, but also of the larger society. How are we to think of GAAP theologically? We will come back to this pertinent question in chapter 9 after we have laid the groundwork for a theological framework for an analysis and interpretation of money.

By theological framework I mean the crafting of a perspective to enable us to grasp the whole of the meaning of money, grasp the *ratio* of money, not its *techne*, that is, the logic and interaction of particulars. We will endeavor to understand the meaning of money within the global meaning of being a person, a being-in-communion. We will follow the route of the social

---

4. Stackhouse's email to this author on September 20, 2008.

trinitarian conception of God to understand personhood, the possibilities of being human, the freedom to transcend the given, and thrusts to be in communion. In the theological discussions that begin in chapter 4, social trinity is always presupposed as the backdrop, the context within which our understanding of personhood and theology of money is constituted.

Within the notion of personhood as being in communion as informed by the intrinsic relationality of the triune God, we aim to forge a perspective that gives us a sense of the whole (*ratio*) of person and insights into the care of the whole. Personhood and social trinity in this book stands as reference and sense. Reference is about role, significance of "particulars in the context of particulars."[5] Sense or meaning is what "renders something intelligible."[6] So here the meaning of personhood is "taken to be its pointing"[7] to the trinitarian communion, the temporal to the eternal, its openness to the triune relationality. The ultimate meaning of personhood is its journey and practices that approximate the mutuality of the Godhead: the growth of personhood toward perichoresis, while the significance of money and monetary systems—and for that matter human institutions—is "one of fostering, nurturing this growth."[8] Chapter 4 begins to tackle some of these issues as it attempts to forge an understanding of the meaning and role of money in terms of enabling people to become both the agent and end of their flourishment.

Exercises

1. Using the information and data provided in the financial statements in this chapter calculate the current ratio of Andover-Newton Hill Church.

2. What are the three reports that SFAS 116 and 117 require churches to produce?

3. What is the relationship between the Statement of Financial Position and the Statement of Revenues, Expenses, and Other Changes in Net Assets?

---

5. Kohák, "Philosophical Biography," in Kohák, *Jan Patočka*, 123.
6. Ibid.
7. Ibid.
8. Ibid.

Chapter 4

Money, Meaning, and Well-Being

"Defining 'Development for Real Life'"

Introduction

WE ENDED CHAPTER 3 with a promise to begin laying the foundation for a theology of money. What kind of theology of money is best suited to the sense and sensibility of ministerial leadership? Sure, a generic theology of money will not serve the interest of those who are engrossed in meaning making, perplexed by money's mystery, yet concerned with the well-being of their congregation and society. What kind of framework do we offer them to make sense of meaning, money, and well-being in a coherent, consistent, and integrated understanding?

As if these concerns are not enough, there are issues and tissues of wider economic relationship that inform ministers' concern about meaning, money, and well-being. In the age of finance, in this post-2008 crash of global financial market, economic development cannot be taken for granted, especially when we have all learned that much of the financial activities that led to the crash were not connected to hard, material economic activities. In this kind of environment, how do the issues and connections between meaning, money, and well-being relate to real development?

Early in 2011 a colleague of mine at Boston University School of Theology offered me a chance to reflect on all these questions. She invited me to speak to her MDiv class on money and development. Based on the pulse and interest of her students and the nature of the course, she formulated the title of this chapter for my participation in her class. She captured in this one topic the interest of not only her students, but also ministers when it comes to their theological interest in money in the post-2008 crash world that still has to deal with the urgent issues of poverty and economic development.

Deciphering the Title

Let us start in a very simple way by examining the title of the lecture that my Boston University colleague asked me to deliver to her students. The middle term of the primary title suggests that the other two terms are ways of expressing meaning. Note the perceived centrality of meaning to development: money, meaning, and wellbeing. This centrality is very instructive.

Meaning as the bridge between money and well-being both separates and connects money and well-being. Though meaning is juxtaposed with money in the title, it is something not marketable or exchangeable as the latter. What is meaning? It is participation in project(s) of worth or sociality bigger than the individual that gives him or her a sense of destiny or purpose. It is our longing for the good itself. It is the longing to participate in the infinite and in community. Meaning is our search for fulfillment. Meaning is about the urge of human beings to fulfill themselves, to actualize their potentialities in directness toward God, the source of being and the good itself. Meaning is about end, the telos of our lives and social existence. Money as a means is used to fulfill the demands of meaning and meaning stands in judgment of it.

Money as a means of exchange reinforces the idea of meaning as an entirely different kind of idea, operation, or praxis and at the same time money announces that without it persons cannot participate in the economic life that undergirds meaning. Meaning is also separate from well-being, but without meaning well-being is severely etiolated.

There is also a subtitle to consider: "Defining 'Development for Real Life.'" So how does money and meaning, and meaning and well-being relate to development for real life? Money and meaning are necessary components of the well-being of those seeking development. The combination of money and meaning is the *technology* of well-being. In an expanded sense, it means that we not only approach well-being through what we make of money and meaning, but also well-being itself is formed by the way of money and meaning.

Money, Meaning, and Well-Being

There is another interpretation: the positive interaction of money, meaning, and well-being as a metaphor for real development. That is, the correct manner of managing money, meaning, and well-being in the micro-setting point to or add to the development of the larger, macro, national sphere. If this second interpretation of the title is the right one, it means we are viewing money, meaning, and well-being as a model and not a technology of development as the first interpretation.

All this, money, meaning, and well-being, is supposed to enable us to understand development. Development is freedom; is about the creation of an environment for action (in the Hannah Arendt's sense), for the "who" of a person to emerge, for a person to be all that he or she can be. It is about creating a society where individuals can actualize their God-given potentials as they act both as means and end of their development. At the minimum, development involves the creation of possibilities for community and participation by all its members so that their potentialities can be drawn out for the common good. A community should be adjudged good because it allows its people to develop their potentialities in the pursuit of an ever-greater common good. How well a community does this will depend on how it allows individuals to develop their unique traits, capabilities, and potentialities and on how well these individual endowments are related to each other in the pursuit of the common good. A good development process is one that is adept at combining these two opposite tendencies or processes: a movement toward uniqueness counterbalanced by a movement toward union.

Economic development is the process of actualizing the potentialities of human beings so that their communities can establish and sustain flourishing human life. This process principally (but not only) courses through the community's conceptualization and practices of work, *excellence*,[1] money, time, and freedom.[2] The social practices of these areas or dimensions of corporate existence condition the kind of social space a society enacts to enable or hinder people as they seek the meaning of their lives, seek social immortality, soul immortality, or eternal life, and strive to initiate

---

1. For the meaning of excellence, see my *Principle of Excellence*.

2. In four of my books I have not only clarified the meanings of these but I have also shown how economic development is specifically related to decisions and policies that affect each of them. Together this body of work throws some light on what I think theology (liberatory philosophy) of development should look like in the twenty-first century. The books are *God and Money* (2008), *Depth and Destiny of Work* (2008), *Principle of Excellence* (2009), and *Ethics and Time* (2010).

something new. In sum, development is about creating and enabling people to live a flourishing existence. It is about achieving some form of *eudaimonia*, blessedness, or flourishing. Money, meaning, and well-being, when they are properly and dynamically integrated, constitute a model of development, if not development itself. So for the rest of the chapter I will focus on money, meaning, and well-being as a way of being for human flourishing.

There is a part of the subtitle that we have to bring into focus before we concentrate on the money, meaning, and well-being. We want to know what kind of development is for real life. The key question here is what is the "real"? The real is about the dynamics, the power, of transformation. It is a way of being for development, the pursuit of the principle of persistent creative realizations of human potentialities for its own sake.[3] It is the freedom to initiate something new amid ongoing social automatism. This way of thinking of development goes against the grain of modern "bureaucratic" thinking on economic development.

Contemporary economic science has settled comfortably into the technocratic management of economies. The constant and reliable has come to dominate the novel and the dynamic. In the technocratic conception of development, faith in the power of political subject is not faith in a revolutionary event. Development, in fact, is only a negative assertion: the social order does not die; it does not change. In a non-technocratic conception, development is a positive assertion: the whole system, which has really died a thousand deaths by exclusions and marginalization, is (or can be) resurrected by a new act of creation orchestrated by agents subject to the good, truth, and beauty of *excellence*.[4]

This orientation to economic development only reflects the nature of politics in many places in the world. Today, politics is no longer about re-constituting the social order or developing a new structure for justice. Politics has long passed the era when it was about starting a new *praxis* from a point (or moments) of social dysfunction in the system in order to move society to an alternative path. Alas, it is no longer about unfolding being as a consequence of subjects' decisions about liberating and life-enhancement potentials, but it is all about positing being as a manipulation

---

3. Adams, *Theory of Virtue*, 89–91, for an argument about how concern for the good of persons is linked with caring for some activities for their own sake.

4. I have borrowed the rhetorical flourish of Oscar Cullman in a different context for my purpose here. Cullman et al, *Immortality and Resurrection*, 19. For the meaning of excellence, see my *Principle of Excellence*.

of institutional and bureaucratic practices. Politics is no longer about encountering the *real*. Modern political science has inaugurated a forgetting of the *real* behind current forms of sociality and behind all sources of new solution.

But we must re-understand politics as the possibility of change in every social order—insofar as change is understood as an openness to the "unfinishedness" of life and the emergence of new alternatives. In doing this, we must not reject the management orientation of politics, but we have to redefine and expand it to incorporate the management of novelty and concentration on possibility for perpetual orientation to the enrichment of life. The pursuit of this good must not be totally severed from a transcendent source or norm, as such a move can become a serious threat to life or being-in-common. Development must be committed to respecting the inherent human dignity and equality of all citizens (as bearers of God's image and as people endowed with the right and duty to participate in the common good) and creating the conditions of possibility necessary for safeguarding human dignity. Development projects or agents of a state's development projects should not act in ways that block the unfolding of potentialities and the promises of God in the lives of persons or social groups.

On the whole, the force of the subtitle, the "real life" portion of it, demands that we think of development or money, meaning, and well-being as a dimension of the new, the emergence of the new. It is here that we will begin our theological journey today. We will focus on Paul Tillich's christological theory of Jesus as the *New Being* to organize our thought about money, meaning, and well-being. Jesus is the *New Being*, is the person who actualized *all* his potentialities and was totally directed to the infinite. Actualization of potentialities and the will-to-the-infinite are crucial dimensions of the development for real life.

Jesus as the New Being and Economic Development

New Being, as Tillich used the term, is about the full realization of human potentialities in a towardness or orientation to the Infinite, God. Development is thus located in the pursuit of *New Beingness*, and in this a resemblance to Jesus as the Christ.[5] The idea of (real) development as interpreted through the lens of New Being poses a challenge to all human beings. Be a

---

5. This is not the time or place for an elaborate treatment of Tillich's notion of Jesus as the New Being. For a lengthier treatment, see Wariboko, *Principle of Excellence*, 97–111.

new being! As Tillich puts it, the New Being happens when humans are able to work out their "essential" nature under the conditions of existence. Even though living under the conditions of historical existence, Jesus showed what humans are essentially, and therefore might be under the conditions of existence.[6] At one point when Jesus was asked if he was the Messiah, the "New Being," he pointed his questioners to his works of transforming human's historical existence. "[The] being of the Christ is his work and that his work is his being, namely the New Being which is his being."[7] If Tillich is correct, there is a sense in which our works, economic development endeavors express and even point beyond our current historical being, to our potential New Being as an historical reality.

My key interest in turning to the notion of New Being is to show that a Christian commitment to development involves a commitment to development as an expression of the *real*. Some of you may have already noticed from the above description of the *real* the potential connections between the notion of Jesus as the New Being and real economic development. But let me be more explicit. In doing this, let us bracket out Tillich's notion of Being as the power of being, "the primal positive force, which is opposed to the negative principle, to the possibility of non-Being."[8] Instead, we will focus on the concept of the New and show not only why he attached it to Being, but also demonstrate its importance to a theological-philosophical understanding of development.

According to Tillich, the New appears in three aspects: as creation, as restoration, and as fulfillment. The new as creation focuses on actualization of potentials, the appearance of unique, actualized existent in history, in the life process. The New as restoration is about how something old can give birth to the something new. It is a rebirth. The New as fulfillment is the experience of the eschatological new, "the expectation of a complete union of the essential and the existential" and it "goes out beyond the limits of time and space."[9]

While Tillich used the concept of New Being, among other purposes, to explain the ideas of God, redemption, and fulfillment,[10] I will apply it to economic development as informed by Hannah Arendt's concepts of freedom, natality, and action. At least in crucial part, development is

6. Tillich, *Systematic Theology*, 2:86–96.
7. Tillich, *Systematic Theology*, 2:168.
8. Tillich, "New Being," 164.
9. Ibid., 166, 167.
10. Ibid., 169–79.

development by virtue of the fact that the individual is genuinely seen as the new that comes into history, she is honored and valued because of her newness and uniqueness,[11] and is supported to develop her capabilities in ways that will un-conceal and establish the "who" of her person in the *polis*. Or to use the words of theologian Robison B. James in his summary of Tillich's notion of the New, "we may say that this individual, whoever she may be, is valued, loved, and cherished, not or not only because she repeats something universal and well-known, and not or not only because she embodies this or that recognized object of everyone's desire, but because she is the singular, unrepeatable person that she is."[12] She is supported, honored, and valued because of her inherent capacity to begin something new in the world. We are close here to the notion of development for real life, the idea of development for real individual life as a bearer of the *imago Dei* and as a participant in the New Beingness of Jesus Christ. To participate in Christ, to be "in Christ" is not an isolated, individual endeavor. It is to participate in the life of people, in Emmanuel, "God with us." This participation in the life of Christ is a dimension of the overall social relations that envelope all persons in the development process. Money is always and everywhere a crucial dimension of social relations. Indeed, money is a social relation.

Money as Social Relation

I conceptualize money as a social relation. Not only are monetary transactions embedded in social relations, but also social relations are constitutive of money itself. I have adequately demonstrated this in my 2008 book, *God and Money*.[13] I will only summarize its lengthy argument in eight points here. First, money is a social institution dependent on state structures and coercive powers of taxation. Second, money is a credit or claim and is thus constituted by social relations. The essential property of "money in general" is social relation. Third, money is not just a convenient medium of exchange, "moneyness" is conferred on any item that answers to the *money of account*.[14] Fourth, money is discursively constructed. There are many

---

11. I owe the construction of the parenthetical phrase to James, "Historicizing God," 15.
12. Ibid.; italics in the original.
13. Wariboko, *God and Money*, 73–122.
14. Let us define money of account along with monetary media for easy understanding. Unit of account or money of account is the abstract numeraire, the official currency. In the United States the money of account is the dollar. "The money of account provides the accounting system in which prices are calculated." Dodd, "Reinventing Monies in

objects that can be used as money forms and each of them have an infinite number of attributes and what leads a society to recognize some properties of objects and declare those that possess them as money media is not a neutral decision. "The functions of money are socially assigned to *objects*."[15]

Fifth, money is simultaneously a social relation and a *relational-thing*. This combination is significant in understanding the social practice of money. Sixth, my concept of money also incorporates Weberian sociological theories to show that prices, inflation, and deflation may be dependent on "class struggle." According to Weber, inflation and deflation are not mere occurrences but are "always in very complex ways dependent on its [money] scarcity" and on the economic struggle for existence, and the balance of power in the actual processes of production and control of money.[16] Seventh, a stable money-space rests on the authoritative foundations of sovereign political and social bases. Thus, money is not only an "economic" phenomenon but also a socio-political phenomenon. Finally, money has multiple meanings and different money has different character depending on the social context in which the transaction is done. "Money is neither culturally neutral nor socially anonymous, but values and social relations reciprocally transform money by investing it with meaning and social patterns."[17]

The conceptualization of money as social relation enables us to think about the connection between money, meaning, and well-being in ways that are not common in the development field. It also enables us to link the discussion of economic development to the dynamic relations of the triune God in the communion of the Godhead. There is no subordination, no supremacy, no privileges, but mutuality, transparency, and perichorectic sociality in the divine Godhead. For understanding the most developed

---

Europe," 558–83, quote p. 563. *Monetary media* relate to the medium, the objects that are used as money. The money of account can be embodied in various material forms like metal coins, paper, or credit cards. The dollar, the money of account, is embodied in a range of objects: gold and silver coins, greenbacks, credit cards, various kinds of e-money, etc. The two qualities or properties of money can be seen in this way: "The first [the money of account] being the title or description and the second [monetary media] the thing that answers to the description." Hart, *Money in an Unequal World*, 248. (This is a description he borrowed from Maynard Keynes.)

15. Ganssman, "Book Review, Geoffrey Ingham," 32; italics in the original.
16. Weber, *Economy and Society*, 78–80, 107–9, 183.
17. Zelizer, *Social Meaning of Money*, 18.

Christian view of positive relations and relationships the logical place to look is the trinitarian language of the Christian tradition, social trinity.

Through this connection to social trinitarianism we can develop a particular relational theology that not only informs the whole framework of development, but also enables us to discern the relational principle of coherence that posits a primarily just, close, and irreducible relations in the economic life of society. What kind of economic development promotes fellowship and encourages the growth of community of nations without privileges and without subjugation?

Money, Meaning, and Well-being

Now that we have gotten some sense of the connection between money and social relations, let us try to explicate how meaning is implicated in the social practice of money. Meaning expresses the urge of a person to fulfill him or herself, to actualize his or her potentials. The economic view of money as mere tool ignores a crucial point. Meaning *(purpose) determines ends and only then the means.* Sociologists and economists may separate means from *meaning* in their analyses or the temporality of production and exchange may give the impression that means and reasoning about means are separated from *meaning* and reason. But they are not really separated. This is so because means is used to fulfill the demands of *meaning*.

For one to step into the social practice of money (to engage in exchange) without *meaning* is to wholly objectivize oneself and block the path to all sensuous interpersonal relationships—both of these are impossible to do. If the *social practice (relation) character* of money is neglected, not only the social meaning of money is impossible to understand, but also money as a realm where the divine Spirit of God can impact and transform individual and social lives becomes difficult, if not, impossible to conceive.

When we spend money we are not only participating in the set of production, distribution, and consumption activities that constitute the "ground of being of money," we are also involved in meaning making, which is to say our engagement in projects of worth. We are engaged in the weaving and reweaving of the social fabric that constitutes and sustains social existence and progress of life. If the *meaningful character* of money or economic transaction of money is neglected, an irrationalistic financialism ("casino capitalism") transforms economic exchange into heteronomous subjection, an external agency capable of granting economic life or death to human sociality. If the meaningful character of money is neglected, a rationalistic, dispassionate invisible hand transforms all agents' decisions into mere revelation of information or mere making of distinctions only of price and quantity in the market. When money is separated from the overall meaning making structure of society, the communality that is relevant for our individual and social well-being comes under severe attack, and the dynamic alignment of society's long and short orientations (or structures) that makes for development for real life suffers.

Thus, an important key for initiating development for real life is a monetary system that will nudge the structures and organization of economic life toward creating and maintaining an embracing economic community that brings *unity-in-difference* into perpetual play and also fosters more ethical relationality without stifling its creativity and galvanizing force.[18] In this regard let us think of an imaginative alternative to the national and global monetary systems that is likely to foster better justice in economic relations. Let us work for an alternative that can secure for individuals and poor countries better participation and integration in an embracing global economic community.

Conclusion

Let me put this chapter in the larger context of the work of an ethicist focusing on economic issues. As an economic theologian what this writer aspires to achieve is to show how theological categories are useful to understanding economics and interpreting economies. For example, we have seen here how the concept of Jesus as the New Being helps to define the meaning of economic development for us. As an economic ethicist this writer also works to clarify how economic concepts and reasoning can be employed to enrich theological-ethical constructions. In this regard, we have also seen how the economic concept of money as a social relation challenges us to develop an adequate theology of relation for economic development.

This writer's abiding interest in working at the intersection of theology and economics is to offer a third option to views offered by both disciplines. This third option is not a syncretism of the two others such that it is a third "something," a *tertium quid* that does not traverse the difference between them. The third option is better conceived as a *coinherence*: it interpenetrates and animates them by a dynamic principle as it goes beyond them.

18. See my 2008 *God and Money*.

The two have their *proton* and *eschaton* in the third, so that the *diastêma* between them is traversed and bridged within it. At the level of scholarship, if this writer is successful there will be a common, bridging frame of discourse, a creative mutual space of interdisciplinarity, between theology and economics. At the level of practical management, the goal is to bring economic actors and national policymakers to the point where thinking, feeling, and acting as economic agents is tantamount to thinking, feeling, and acting theonomously.

Chapter 5

Budgeting and Pro-Forma Statements

Introduction

In the United States the making of the federal government budget is a very acrimonious and contentious process. People are so committed to their own projects and party ideology that they will not compromise on spending cuts or raising of taxes to cover deficits. The kind of dogged commitments shown during recent budget fights led a politician to say: "It is a budget and not theology." While it is true that fights over budgetary allocations are not exactly theological debates or matters of eternal life, it is truer to say that budget is theology. Budgets allow agencies and persons to institutionalize their vision in the way a community's collective revenues are allocated. The allocation of money in a polity signifies certain political and ethical commitments and point to what a people or group affirms and values as important and worthy of financial commitment.

In this vein, the budget of a church points to its deepest commitments. The budget as an indicator of the economic power of the church expresses its concept of what it means to do the work of Christ, to witness the Gospel, or execute the "greatest and holiest work of the Church." The budget expresses the mission of the church. The budget of a church could be seen as the way the congregation is attempting to effect a passage from its abstract, spiritual theological commitments to their embodied, concrete realization. In this understanding of budget, the basic dialogue and practice of monetary allocations are of special concern. And in that context a question arises: How does the crossing of the boundary between theological commitments to practical socio-ethical engagement influence the shape and

Budgeting and Pro-Forma Statements

interactions between the various functions of the church and ultimately the "habit of the heart" of the congregation?

Preparation of Budgets

With that preface to budgeting, let us turn to the issues relating to preparing a budget. Preparing a budget is about projecting monetary allocations into the future. It is what is also sometimes called doing a pro-forma analysis. The experts can prepare either one-year or multi-year pro-forma statements. There are basically two ways of preparing budgets or pro-forma statements: The first method is predicting one line item at a time. Here you predict the level of all line items in the Statement of Revenue, Expenses, and other changes in Net Assets. The prediction may start with the assumption of an erased slate from the previous years and thus the necessity and justification of allocation of resources to each line has to be made afresh, from scratch. This approach is what is called *zero-based budgeting*. This is very cumbersome and it is not necessarily more authentic than the other approach.

The second method is to predict what the overall level of the budget will be. Once this number is known and its relative percentage increase or decrease over the previous year, you adjust each line upward or downward by the same percentage. This method is called *incremental budgeting*. Both the zero-based or incremental budgeting approach can function either at the level of line item or programs. Either the finance committee examines and allocates funds on the basis of line items or on the basis of church programs (each program with its own line items) in the Revenue and Expense Statement.

In both approaches the most important and also the most difficult to predict is how each item or program will change or behave in the coming year. For instance, how well can you predict total contributions (pledges, offerings, contributions, etc)? If you get the revenue number wrong you are off track immediately, as it will not only affect the expenses and revenue-expense margin, but also net assets and balance sheet. In predicting revenue, you may want to consider past growth rate for five years and then project forward. Contribution is often cyclical. Hence you may want to consider the relationship between contributions and what is happening in the overall economy. Note that contribution is also a function of the kind of programs the church is running and the introduction or elimination of programs may make the overall contribution number deviate from the trend rate.

Many accountants when predicting expenses will use the *common-size adjustment technique*. They take note of the historical percentage of expense item to revenue, and on the basis of this forecast the expense number. Alternatively, they predict the growth rate of the expense line item. The common-size adjustment technique will give a better prediction if the church expense structure is dominated by variable cost. But if fixed cost is substantially a larger component of cost than variable cost, the growth in individual line will work better.

Whatever method is used it is important to always compare budgeted revenues and expenses to the actual numbers. This will serve to flag and track deviations from the projected path and also as a study in improving the forecasting skills of the pastor or the committee.

I have provided this simple discussion of the budgeting process and technique so that you as the pastor or the would-be pastor will understand the work done by your finance committee. You do not need to be an expert; you only need an appreciation of the committee's work and how to engage with the process theologically and as a leader of the congregation. As a leader of the parish, congregation, or church you need a "theory of budget" to guide your reasoning and the occasional well-meaning "fights" over the various "allocation pots."

The Pastor's Theory of the Budget

Every church or finance committee has a perspective (whether declared or implied) that guides what it does and how it does it—how it allocates the annual resources of the church. The opportunities it recognizes and appropriates, how it solves the problems it encounters, and the problems it finds and solves are given meaning within a particular framework. The perspective—premises for decisions, assumptions about the populace from which it draws its members and resources, the religious environment, communication channels, members and non-members, and competitors (other churches or religions)—is the frame of reference for its budgeting activities. When this mindset, paradigm is clear, focused, consistent, and fits reality, it becomes a propelling and sustaining force for success. Otherwise, it becomes an inhibiting force. Seen in this way, the perspective of a church is its most powerful force (apart from the Spirit of God) and explains both its success and the challenges the church as an organization faces. In fact, the set of assumptions that shapes and guides its behavior and defines its

Budgeting and Pro-Forma Statements

decisions, fashion its interpretation of its world and conditions what results it considers meaningful is its *theory of the church*. And it is also the theory of the budget.

Budgets are powerful instruments for the mission of churches when they fit their theories of the church. Alert and dynamic churches are constantly redefining their modus operandi, modus vivendi, and their budgets. The budgeting process and allocations are strategic means of regenerating their core mission and recreating themselves to fit the demands of their theory of the church. The budgeting process, which should be inclusive and consensus-building as much as possible, is one way a church should test its assumptions about its (1) specific mission, (2) religious, social, political, and economic environment, and (3) the core competences, capabilities, relationships, and services needed to accomplish its mission.

The assumptions of the pastor leading or tele-guiding this budgeting process should not be driven by needs of the current economic (socio-political) conditions alone. She has to develop a point of view about the future and about the future of Christianity. She also needs to know that the budgeting process of a church should not start with money, but only end with it. To make this point clearer let me resort to the story of Jesus Christ feeding five thousand men and unnamed number of women and children as recorded in Mark's gospel:

> So they went away by themselves in a boat to a solitary place. But many who saw them leaving recognized them and ran on foot from all the towns and got there ahead of them. When Jesus landed and saw a large crowd, he had compassion on them, because they were like sheep without a shepherd. So he began teaching them many things. By this time it was late in the day, so his disciples came to him. "This is a remote place," they said, "and it's already very late. Send the people away so that they can go to the surrounding countryside and villages and buy themselves something to eat." But he answered, "You give them something to eat." They said to him, "That would take more than half a year's wages! Are we to go and spend that much on bread and give it to them to eat?" "How many loaves do you have?" he asked. "Go and see." When they found out, they said, "Five—and two fish." Then Jesus directed them to have all the people sit down in groups on the green grass. So they sat down in groups of hundreds and fifties. Taking the five loaves and the two fish and looking up to heaven, he gave thanks and broke the loaves. Then he gave them to his disciples to distribute to the people. He also divided the two fish among them all. They all ate

> and were satisfied, and the disciples picked up twelve basketfuls of broken pieces of bread and fish. The number of the men who had eaten was five thousand. (Mark 6:32–44 NIV.)

I want to interpret this story in the light of the theology of accounting and money that we are crafting in this book. I want us to specifically examine it to discover what it can tell us about the theological or philosophical perspective we need to bring to the budgeting process in the church. In order to avoid discussing every project or program that the budget of a church funds let us limit our discussion to the part of the budget that helps the poor in need. For the purposes of proceeding let us assume that there are three material ways of helping the poor overcome poverty. One, the church can continually give money to them as often as they need it. The problem with this approach is that it does not move the recipients forward toward self-sustenance and independence. We run the risk of turning them into dependents in the long run.

The second approach runs like this and it is best delivered in a parable that Father Eddy Lundemba Makuta, one of my former students from Congo, told me. According to the parable, a philosopher and his students went to the countryside and saw a poor farmer, his wife, and children living on a hilltop. They depended on a malnourished cow for milk for their sustenance. The philosopher told his students that as long as the cow was alive and meeting the needs of the family at the bare, subsistence level the husband has no motivation to seek for an improved lifestyle for his family. He asked one of the students to push down the cow from the top of the hill. The cow died. The man was forced to come down and look for work in the factory at the foot of the hill. His income level changed and the family living standards improved. This approach seems cruel and forced the family into industrial labor without seeking their opinion. Besides, no incentive was given to the family to be creative with the malnourished cow, their existing resource. The philosopher and his students did not investigate or work with the family to make the cow multiply or be more fruitful.

The third approach to helping the poor is to take what they have, work together with them to be creative with it, and show or help them to multiply it. The emphasis here is on creativity, capabilities, and how to help people be both the agents and goal of their own development. Jesus's approach to solving the needs of the hungry crowd falls into this third category—at least this is how I am interpreting Mark 6:32–43 for the limited purpose of this book. It should be noted that I am only interpreting the passage in a managerial and strategic sense and my exercise should not be construed as a denial of its spiritual message.

There are nine lessons we can take from this story of the feeding of the five thousand. First of all Mark (in verse 34) tells us that Jesus had compassion on them. He recognized their vital need for nourishment at that crucial moment in the deserted place. Compassion involves care and going beyond oneself. According to philosopher Martha Nussbaum, it is a painful emotion occasioned by an awareness of another person's suffering and misfortune. It is an evaluative judgment on the person's condition and there is a double (you and the person) feeling of pain. It is an emotion that provokes or motivates actions to help the sufferer out of his or her bad situation.[1] But compassion is not enough if it is not backed up by concrete actions. The form of action a church needs to take to ameliorate the conditions of the sufferer needs to be carefully thought through.

Second, note that the solution did not start with money, but with what people had in their hands. The disciples thought of the financial endowment it would take to feed the huge crowd. But Jesus asked the disciples to find out what the people had. They had five loaves and two fish. These they gave to Jesus and he multiplied them. Note the sense of creativity here. The existing meager resources they gave Jesus were the basis of the miracle.

This brings us to our third lesson. Jesus performed a miracle, the wonder of multiplication. Today, not many pastors or finance committees can multiply loaves and fish. So where is the miracle going to come from? Our miracles today are sourced from our technology, education, and training. They are in a sense alternative sources of miracles. The church can use its access to technology, education, and training to help the poor within this country or outside. For instance, how can the church harness easily available technology in this country to aid the poor in other countries increase their own resources? When you train a man to fish and also to increase his fish stock instead of giving him fish every time he asks for it, you have done a miracle for him. When you enable a woman to acquire education and skills, you have given her the wonderful resources of independence and knowledge necessary to both navigate her world and support her family. Of course, all this should be done from the humble position that human technology is not the source of our salvation and the church, especially an economically rich nation should not put its hope on the magic of modern science and technology.

1. Nussbaum, *Upheavals in Thought*, 297–353.

Accounting and Money for Ministerial Leadership

The fourth lesson relates to partnership. The kind of work necessary to perform the "miracles" we have suggested here calls for partnership. It demands a partnership between the haves and the almost-have-nots. Note that I did not say have-nots. In approaching people to help them we must not assume that they have nothing to offer in the process of their own emancipation and development. They may even say they have nothing, but we need to press further to discover their peculiar "jar of oil" like the widow of the prophet in 2 Kings 4:1–7. Elisha blessed the jar of oil and the oil was multiplied. She sold the oil and lived on the income that remained after paying off her debts.

My emphasis on the need to work with the poor by incorporating their own resources, talents, and time should not be construed to mean that I am oblivious of the fact that the very physical and social conditions of the poor are often hostile to any meaningful partnership. Mark's story hints at this when we read that the people were in a desolate or deserted place. Nonetheless, Jesus performed his miracle with what the people supplied him. So we too must try to forge partnership no matter the hostility under which we work. And this is our fifth lesson.

The sixth lesson is that the solution or "development" Jesus provided is internally generated. The bread and fish came from the people. Jesus did not command sustenance to fall down as manna from heaven. Let the church do its technological miracle with what the people or the poor are willing to put into its hand. The church needs to find out what the poor have on hand that can be incorporated into their own development and flourishment. They might not have much, but we must strive to enable them to participate in their own development. Someone once said a good general goes to war with the army he has, not the one he wishes to have. We work with the poor according to what they have, not with what we think they must have.

Seventh, Jesus asked them to form groups. This signals the beginning process of cooperation and the knowing of one another. When he asked them to sit in groups and they obeyed and sat in groups, he converted strangers to neighbors. The sitting together and the subsequent miracle that ensued suggest that people could be more creative with the little they have when they cooperate and work under God's guidance and wisdom. My thinking is that projects in the church must be aimed at building or strengthening social harmony or the fabric of society.

The next lesson we need to note is that the approach of Jesus created surplus. After all the men, women and children ate twelve basketfuls of

Budgeting and Pro-Forma Statements

fragments were carried away. These fragments could be food for some after their immediate needs have been met. It could also be seen as investment, seed for future use. Here we see that the satisfaction of needs moves beyond the present into the future. So my question is: Is the church helping the poor in a way that provide seeds for them for future investment or bread for future sustenance?

Finally, Jesus's approach does the work of the two other approaches to aiding the poor. But it does it in a different way. Like the others, the needs of the poor are met and there is a new source or insight on how to create sustenance. It is a partnership within the context of mutuality and communion and creates a trajectory for the poor to regain their confidence, creativity, and dignity.

Jesus's approach to the feeding of the five thousand makes a crucial point about his ministry, helping the poor and marginalized, and those in need. He "allocated" his very powerful resources, the power of miracle, to serve the people. The story portrayed the spirit of his earthly ministry: compassion and building harmony, among others. Today money is one of the church's valuable resources and the minister should ensure that its allocation and use reflect the spirit of her ministerial leadership and church's mission. "Even though money and spirit are quite different realities, no one will claim that they have no relation to each other."[2]

Indeed, budgeting is the concrete, incontrovertible expression of the organizational "spirit" of leadership and governance in monetary language. Budgeting is the care of the soul or spirit of leadership. It is a veritable locus of a pastor's relationship to the responsibilities to the mission of Christ and the site of struggle against degeneration of ministerial leadership and its orientation, intent, and forward thrust. When budgets support ministerial leadership in this way it is good.

Despite the importance of budgeting in expressing the mission of a church, it is a very limited range of engagement with the vital issues of our contemporary monetary systems. It deals with the *stock of money*. Budgets are not about the production, circulation, and control of money supply in an economy—the *flows of money*. We require new kind of studies that can shine a bright theological-ethical light on the motion of money at both national and global spheres so as to highlight the serious ethical and theological issues that pertain to the production, circulation, control, and use of money in the global structures and organizations of economic life.

2. Bühlmann, foreword, xi.

Theology in Motion 5: Life in Money and Accounting

Money has a certain analogy with life and it has sometime been crudely described as the life-blood of the economy. Once we grasp this: that is, the idea that money is not a *dead matter*, not a "dead identity," but a pulsating flow of energy in the economy, we realize that theological treatments of money up to now have been very inadequate. Theologians and theological ethicists have often treated money as a matter, not as a form of energy, not as a flow. The stock concept of money and the related ethical issues dealing with the allocation and use of the quantity of money in a given political economy have dominated the theological discourse and not much has been done on the analysis of money as a *motion* (the flow concept of money). Theologians and ethicists have tarried too long in one spot; concentrating too much on giving and generosity and individual ethics to the neglect of social and systemic issues. In so doing they have largely ignored the production, circulation, and control of money, the flows of money, which actually determine who gets what quantity, when and how.

In general, theological analyses show one or both of two problems. First, often little or nothing is said about structures and organization of the monetary relations that condition the ethical responses of Christians. There is also silence on how the content of some fundamental Christian values and doctrines might influence the possible reorganization of the structures of the monetary life.

Second, they ignore the highly important dual nature of money. By the dual nature, I mean that there are two sides to money. Money is a flow, and money is a stock. The two are one—there are no two natures of money, but one. Money is a dialectical identity of these two sides. Whether viewed from stock or flow perspective, you are looking at one and the same phenomenon. It is like the famous ambiguous duck-rabbit drawing by the American Gestalt psychologist Joseph Jastrow. From one point of view it is a series of flows and events; from another point it is a stock. It is just a shifting perspective on one and the same object. It is not two objects brought together in the form of a synthetic identity. The linear quantity is the embodiment of flows and the flows are the stock in process. The object is not changed, but there are two different takes from two angles of vision. The flow and stock are not parts that add up to a greater whole. It is one complex indivisible whole, with parts that overlap and cohere with one another, that can and must be looked at from multiple standpoints. You cannot get the richness of the subject matter or its theology from only a single standpoint.

But it appears theologians have rested contentedly focusing only on a single perspective.

Owing to this lopsided attention, theological scholarship has focused more on personal moral transformation than on the structures and organization of monetary relations. Also attention has principally been on the redistribution of monetary capital as the solution to national poverty in poor countries—all this to the neglect of the role of structures, dynamics, and function of money creation in the underdevelopment of economies. Thus, there is a dearth of ethical studies on how the logic and dynamics of the global trade and payment system (the monetary systems) impact the economic well-being of the poor regions of the world.

This distinction we have made between stock and flow concepts of money provides philosophical grist for a possible theological analysis of accounting. The itch of accounting is to convert or translate flows into recordable matter. Accounting takes stock of what is an ever-flowing stream of human activities and presents them as a snapshot at a particular moment. But theology of money is not merely about stewardship but also about the flow of human activities that produce, distribute, and allocate money within a nation and across and between nations. When we are engaged in the budgeting process and its accounting practices we run the risk of looking at the church's work with a dead gaze. In trying to pin down flows under the hammer of budgetary pressures we forget that the activities of persons and social practices, which constitute the church, are moving divergently and convergently, separating and uniting simultaneously at the time. Under these circumstances it is easy to forget that budget is about human life, not abstract numbers and that budget *is* theology.

Exercises

1. Discuss the zero-based budgeting process and examine its merits or demerits with regard to your own church's budgeting process.
2. Describe the scriptural or theological framework that informs budgets and budgeting processes in your church.
3. Is the budget of religious organization a theological statement, an expression of deepest moral commitments, or a mere inventory of how future resources will be used? Please give reasons to support your position.

CHAPTER 6

Holy Clarity: Transparency and Internal Controls

Introduction

THERE ARE MANY PASTORS who treat the financial information of their churches as highly classified data. They think that members of the congregation do not have as much a right to the information as themselves. Worse, they think that the information contained in the financial documents might constitute an embarrassment to all parties. This attitude to transparency carries some inevitable costs. Mistrust, misunderstanding, and suspicion are some of the typical results in a church that has a culture of secrecy.

Secrecy and opaqueness may also be symptoms of a leadership that does not understand the importance of evaluation in the running of a church. Evaluation helps us "to find and to create clarity in our organization's sense of purpose, and to see the truth when we investigate the impact of our activities."[1] Financial statements are not mere records of an organization's transactions, but are a veritable tool of evaluation if properly understood and applied. If there is an explicit planning of the financial resources of a church, a well-defined set of goals that informs the sources and uses of funds, and a conscious evaluation of stewardship, then getting clear about financial statements can make a significant difference to leadership practices. As Sarah Drummond puts it: "I believe that clarity is holy and pleasant to God and that any leadership practice that brings greater clarity into institutions that seek to follow God's will is an inherently useful practice."[2]

---

1. Drummond, *Holy Clarity*, xvi.
2. Ibid.

Holy Clarity: Transparency and Internal Controls

How can a pastor be clear about the finances of her church? What must a pastor do for her church to be financially transparent? Let us start from communication. There is an important link between transparency and the pastor's role as the communicator of vital, communitywide information in the church. There are at least three points or dimensions at the intersection of communication and transparency in Christian ministry. The first dimension of communicating financial information is about accuracy and truthfulness. The church must provide the necessary and required financial information and data to its people according to requirements of GAAP. For a pastor operating at this level it is necessary to show that the budgetary allocations, sources of revenue, and expenditure and investment pattern of the church identify with the mission of the church.

At the second dimension of transparency the pastor and the financial committee make the effort to show that budgetary allocations, sources of revenue, and expenditure and investment patterns of the church identify with the mission of the church. The final dimension or level of clarity is reached when allocations, sources, and patterns that constitute the financial structure of the church identify closely with the mission of the church and exceeds the ethos of transparency in the larger corporate world.

The preparation, release, and presentation of a church's financial statements may reflect the standards of GAAP and the mission of the church, but if its level of transparency does not exceed that of the "Pharisee" or the business world then there is no holy clarity.[3] This is necessary not only for churches to earn the public trust, but also to show that as religious organizations they hold themselves to higher standards than what society expects from businesses. The discerning public is not the only constituency that matters in holy clarity. The public-image dimension of clarity will be inadequate without any form of identification with the kingdom of God. Indeed, there is no real holy clarity if a church's gathering and use of economic resources do not reflect the larger perspective of the kingdom of God.

What must a church do if it wants to achieve holy clarity in finance? Here is a listing and discussion of some of the standards of transparency such a church needs to adopt.

---

3. See Drummond, *Holy Clarity*.

Accounting and Money for Ministerial Leadership

Transparency and Evaluation

I will start from an unusual place. When it comes to transparency, books on accounting do not start from practices of evaluation, as their authors do not think that a well-designed evaluation can guide a community or corporate body to greater transparency, clarity. However, this process of clarifying what an organization seeks to accomplish, collecting information that can help assess the impact of its activities, and then engaging in a communal conversation about the findings is what evaluation is all about.[4] Any good transparency program rides on an excellent practice of evaluation. Achieving and communicating financial transparency work best with these conditions: the institutional goals are clear, data (in this case financial data) are properly collected, stored, and analyzed to assess what has been accomplished in a given accounting period, and there is a culture to openly talk about what to do with the accomplishments. These are conditions that a good evaluation practice will put in place in a church.

For a church, evaluation as a way of uncovering truth about its activities and programs, a way of throwing light on the "dark spots" that bred malfeasance, and a way of "seeing" itself. Evaluation in this sense is a form of internal control, which is a mechanism and pathway to effective and efficient leadership. Evaluation is also an integral path of (to) shaping a community's vision and the dynamic work of turning it into actuality.[5] Sarah Drummond's *Holy Clarity* (2009) provides an accessible point of entry to evaluation and planning for those who want to learn more about this important practice of leadership and perhaps adopt it as *way of thinking* rather than viewing it as one more burden to bear.

Audits and Financial Reports

Another standard of transparency that a minister must adhere to is the timely provision of audited current financial statements (statement of financial position, statement of activities, and statement of cash flows, according to SAS 116 and 117) to his or her congregation. The church needs to hire a qualified certified public accountant, CPA, to perform an annual audit of its financial affairs. The annual audit should be done in a timely manner. After a qualified auditor has prepared the financial statements

---

4. Ibid., 1–3.
5. Ibid., 53–77.

the pastor will provide them (including auditor's report and notes to the financial statements) to members of the church upon written request. (This was the normal approach in the past. But in this day of the Internet when the cost of providing information to members has dropped drastically it is important for the church to post these items on its website without waiting for members to make written requests.)

In addition the pastor may also need to provide financial reports of programs and projects. If the church is publicly raising funds for projects, charity, or educational programs it makes sense to provide financial statements and reports to donors who ask for them. On this issue, the wisdom of the Evangelical Council for Financial Accountability (ECFA), "an accreditation agency dedicated to helping Christian ministries earn public trust" is worth quoting at length:

> Financial disclosure is not only an accepted, expected, and required form of accountability in society at large, but it also represents the even higher standard of openness for Christian organizations operating in the forum of the Church. It may be true that public disclosure of financial information is required, in part, to protect the donor public. While this is the reason most often given to justify governmental regulation, the reputation of the Christian ministry in general is at stake.

Public disclosure protects Christian ministry from the danger of claiming ownership of God's gifts. It also protects us from the temptation to acquire assets as our lasting goal. Furthermore, the availability of financial statements promotes responsible Christian stewardship over assets as donors seek to make monetary investments in the work of the Kingdom. Simply put, Christian organizations provide current financial statements to anyone who submits a written request for them because it is the right thing to do.[6]

It is germane to mention that financial information on individual giving and contributions is protected from disclosure. While the church reveals its total contributions it is not required to give the details of contributions of each and every member of the church. Of course, it is a different story if it has taken contributions from government or outside corporate donors for projects and programs. In such a case the financial statements should reveal the sources of the contributions. On the expense side, the financial statements need to show if the church is making "secret payments" to cover up fraud and abuses on the part of its clergy. Still on the expenditure side,

---

6. Evangelical Council, "ECFA Standard 5."

a pastor may also want to reveal her total compensation package instead of burying it under total salary and benefits of staff.

Internal Control Systems

Churches would be wise to institute rigorous and comprehensive internal control systems to effectively record and efficiently manage transactions, safeguard the assets of the church, prevent fraud and financial irregularities, make fraud detection easier, and protect the reputation of ministers against unfounded accusations of financial impropriety. Beyond the issues of financial accounting, organizations generally institute a set of internal control systems to ensure that their organizational objectives are realized and there is proper adherence to management's policies and procedures.

This process of internal control starts with keeping accurate financial records. As David O. Awe, an expert on church accounting puts it:

> A church, like other organizations, employs its limited resources to pursue its mission, which is soul winning. Without accurate records of income and expenses, without a method of measuring how available resources are employed to pursue the mission of the church, it is impossible to know how effectively and efficiently these resources are being employed. It is inconceivable that someone would run his own business with the volume running to hundreds of thousands or sometimes millions of dollars without seeking the help of competent professionals to keep the books. Yet in some churches, we frequently see such actions.[7]

Control System Specifics

Over and beyond the matter of keeping record of transactions there are specific controls that the pastor and the finance committee need to put in place. It is often difficult and demanding to implement the internal control procedures that will ensure the effective and efficient management of a church's resources. Since this book is not written to turn the pastor into an accounting expert we will limit our comments to six key principles of internal control. These are principles that every minister needs to know so as to understand the basics of the internal control systems of her church.

7. Awe, *Accounting*, 74.

Holy Clarity: Transparency and Internal Controls

1. Assets must be properly recorded and safeguarded. There must be enough of a paper trail to trace approval and disbursement of funds. The pastor has the fiduciary responsibility to safeguard the resources of the church, and keeping adequate records is part of fulfilling this responsibility. Let us illustrate the issue of safeguarding the assets of the church with a simple example. When a church acquires an asset, the asset is marked with name or symbol of the church, recorded in the books of the church, and depreciated according to GAAP. When it comes time to sell the asset the finance committee or whoever is authorized to execute the transaction must consult the guides or experts on the current market value of the asset to establish its fair market price. The sales value should not be determined arbitrarily.

2. The function of authorizing transactions, recording them in the books, and keeping custody of the ensuing assets must be handled by separate, unrelated persons in order to make it difficult for one person to commit a crime and cover it up. If it is only one person who collects the offering on a Sunday, records it, and banks it, and then also writes the check, then the principle of segregation of duties is violated and the church has opened itself to potential fraud.

3. There must be a subsystem of verification and reconciliation to ensure that what is recorded is actually what happened. For instance, purchase orders must be reconciled with payments and with the actual goods received. Or, cash counted and recorded after a service or program by one person must be checked against what is deposited in the bank by another. Anytime one person counts the money there is a risk that he or she will pocket some of it and deposit the rest. In this scenario, the deposit record of the church will always match that of the bank when a second person verifies it. It seems like the point of checks and balances should begin by always requiring that two people count and verify the money. This also protects the people doing the counting.

4. The system must be geared toward preventing and detecting frauds and financial irregularities. The pastor, the board, and the finance committee must not rely on trust alone to run the accounting system of the church. There must be systems and programs to reduce opportunities for fraud. There must also be periodic reviews of the systems put in place to prevent fraud.

5. Preventing crime and abuse of office is not only a matter of institutionalizing accounting and audit controls, but also about developing a corporate culture of transparency, honesty, ethical dealing, and openness. In the situation where the leadership of the church hides the financial affairs of the church in a cloak of secrecy and circumvents the rules of the church in awarding contracts they are unwittingly providing rationalizations for individuals with access to the economic resources of the church to commit crimes.

6. The pastor must be knowledgeable and humble enough to know that she needs professional help to set up and run a church internal control system. Most denominations in the United States now publish standards and examples of best practices for their churches and parishes. Let her familiarize herself with the standards and best practices of her denomination.

Offerings and Contributions

Let us now briefly apply some of the rules to the design of a system of handling and recording offerings and contributions. The church must record the contributions made by every individual in order to provide the annual statement of contributions to individuals at year's end. This process is preceded by certain internal control measures. The person or persons collecting the offerings and those counting it must not be one and the same set of persons. Family members or husband and wife should not be part of the same team counting collections. Besides, there should not be fewer than two persons in each team of collectors and counters, and the counters must sign off on the amount collected. The persons involved in collecting and counting offerings must be rotated from time to time or asked to take annual breaks of two to three weeks. This will prevent one person from exercising so much influence and authority over the collecting and counting of offerings such that other members of the church are afraid to ask questions. Besides, it is important to have new persons to crosscheck the entries and records of those before them.

It is also important to count the offering in a secure and private location. Once the counting is done and recorded the collections must be handed over to the treasurer of the church to deposit in the bank. Under no circumstances must collections be spent before they are banked. The financial records and statements relating to the collections must not be kept at the private homes of the treasurer or accountant of the church, but at a secure location in the church or offsite. One advantage of keeping records at an offsite location is that in case of fire or burglary the records of the church will not be totally lost.

Theology in Motion 6: The Philosophy of Internal Control

The philosophy of internal control in accounting has a lot to teach us about how to respond to money and materialism in the United States. The principles of internal control are about stewardship of resources, about what an organization does with them, and what management and staff are to *become* (honest or fraudulent). It is about preserving and promoting the practices of excellence that serves the *goods internal* of the organization and its form of activity. The internal goods are those that can be realized only by participating in the virtue-dependent form of processes and procedures as well as judged by the standards of GAAP, organizational goals, and pastoral excellence.[8] When internal goods are realized they belong to the whole community, further improving its practices of excellence.

The promotion of goods internal works well in an organization that promotes certain kinds of virtues that resist *external goods*. These goods, in contrast to internal goods, include prestige, status, honor, and power and can be achieved without excellence (that is "standards of excellence which are appropriate to, and partially definitive of,"[9] that work of the organization) in the activity in question and when achieved are always some individual's property or possession. According to Alasdair MacIntyre, "external goods are therefore characteristically objects of competition in which there must be losers as well as winners. Internal goods are indeed the outcome of competition to excel, but it is characteristic of them that their achievement is good for the whole community who participates in the practice."[10] MacIntyre also discusses the cultivation of virtues, certain principal moral virtues that enable participants to satisfy the standards of excellence in performance. He defines virtue as "an acquired human quality the posses-

---

8. Here I have borrowed from Alasdair MacIntyre's idea of excellence and internal goods to serve my purpose. MacIntyre, *After Virtue*, 187. See also Stout, *Ethics After Babel*, 267.

9. MacIntyre, *After Virtue*, 187.

10. Ibid., 190–91.

sion and exercise of which tends to enable us to achieve those goods which are internal to practices and the lack of which effectively prevents us from achieving any such goods."[11] Needless to say that the church must cultivate certain virtues, especially those relating to transparency and competence for its internal control systems to work properly.

While every well-designed internal control system works because people are trusted to do the right thing, it also has ways of enabling them to resist the mesmerizing pull of the appeals of mammon. There are rules, regulations, and checks and balances to make it (near) impossible to succumb to the temptations of fraud and malicious destruction of corporate (church) property. And as we have stated earlier a culture of openness and honesty—in general, certain virtues— are necessary to drown out the voices of mammon's invitation or the calls of the Sirens. An internal control system ultimately works because there is an organizational "spirit" or ethos so powerful that in its presence the allure of fraud grows strangely dim.

It is important to mention that the rules and regulations, the spirit and ethos, which together empower the people of the organization to do the right thing exist against the backdrop of the belief or conviction that management and staff are all capable of giving in to the deadly appeal of mammon. This conviction about the "original sin" of human beings in organizations is also the "original sin" of the accounting profession, which many pastors deny at peril to their churches. Unlike pastors, accountants do not fool themselves into believing that church staff, when given the opportunity, will not steal. This is not to say that accountants view everyone as a potential criminal. The assumption they make is for the purpose of designing robust systems of internal controls in organizations.

Given all the preceding discussions, we boldly state that theologically it is important for ministers to consider internal control not as a technique, but as a way of living. All this brings us to Greek mythology about two heroes, Odysseus and Jason, who resisted the deadly appealing calls of the Sirens.[12] Odysseus before starting sail asked his crew to tightly bind him to the mast of the ship and that on no account should they listen to his requests to free him as the ship sails past the island of the Sirens. Indeed as his ship went past the island he heard the irresistible calls of the Sirens and earnestly begged to be released, struggling in his bonds and cursing his oarsmen. His oarsmen

---

11. Ibid., 191.

12. This way of thinking of internal controls in the context of Greek mythology was inspired by Bonk, *Missions and Money*, 188.

did not obey him and thus saved him from certain death. "His method of resistance illustrates the way of bonds and restrictions. It is not pleasant, but it can be effective in saving us from our own desires."[13]

How Jason was saved from the deadly but irresistible appeal of the Sirens is different. As he and his Argonauts sailed past the island of the Sirens, they began to hear the songs of the Sirens and were succumbing to them. But Princess Medea called Orpheus, the Greek god of music who played heavenly music to drown out and counter the sound and deadly pull of the Sirens' songs. Thus Jason and all on board were saved.

This story as Jonathan Bonk interprets it sets before Christians in the midst of the mesmerizing pull of Western materialism three choices of response to the appeal of mammon. "(1) we can give in to its deadly appeal; (2) we can bind ourselves by the rules and regulations that it impossible for us to respond as we would like; (3) or we can drown out the Sirens' invitation to death by listening instead to the music of the Spirit, and by learning to sing God's songs. '... And the things of the earth will grow strangely dim in the light of his glory and grace.'"[14]

By way of reaching conclusion, it is important to state that a well-crafted philosophy and well-executed practice of internal controls brings with it certain benefits. The improvement of excellence in all departments of the church also brings with it certain benefits, among which are safeguards against legal and financial liabilities. In the next chapter, we will discuss some of the potential legal and financial liabilities a church faces when it either breaks the law or runs afoul of its internal control systems.

Exercises

1. How would you describe "holy clarity" with respect to financial accounting?
2. Discuss the key principles of internal controls in accounting.
3. Do you agree or disagree with the author's theological interpretation of internal control in accounting? State why you support or disagree with his views.
4. Describe your understanding of the philosophical and theological connections between financial transparency and holy clarity.

13. Ibid.
14. Ibid.

CHAPTER 7

Liabilities, Compliances, and Good Practices

Introduction

MOST PASTORS WILL EASILY agree that running a church is not a walk in the park. But not many have realized that as leaders of their organizations their actions or inactions expose themselves and their churches to potential liabilities. In order not to bore the reader, who I believe is clergy man/woman or theologian and who has little patience with arcane legal and accounting details, I will provide a simple overview of the potential liabilities that a church faces due to commissions or omissions of its pastors, trustees, and staff. Those interested in more details are advised to seek professional advice. The goal of the discussions below is to raise the awareness of clergy so they would seek advice from lawyers, accountants, and qualified members of their churches and also to communicate better with such professionals.

Employees

When it comes to employee matters two of the most important issues are the proper classification of workers as employees or contractors and compliance with all labor laws. There are many things the church has to do to fully comply with IRS rules and labor laws, but these are some of requirements every pastor or finance committee needs to know:
- Every employee must fill out employment eligibility Form I-9 and should be given a W-2 at the end of every calendar year before January 31 of the New Year. But a contractor will fill out Form W-9 at the

time of its, his, or her engagement. In addition, if the contractor is paid for any service or products the church should give such a person Form 1099 before January 31 of the following year. Any withholding tax which is deducted from employees' compensation or honorarium paid to foreign ministers must be promptly forwarded to the IRS.

A church faces liabilities for the negligent acts of its employees. Also criminal acts performed on its premises by the employees will expose the church to legal and financial liabilities. For instance, if a member of the pastorate, children's department, or a volunteer sexually abuses a child the church will incur huge legal expenses. There is no need to rehash the liabilities that the Catholic Church in America continues to suffer due to the clergy sexual abuse scandal. It is important for churches to screen and conduct background checks on its employees and volunteers before engaging them in the services of the church.

Churches also face liabilities from counseling if it leads to injuries or losses. So it is important for churches to have only those who are well trained in counseling or spiritual guidance to counsel or guide members. It is actually preferable to refer members to professional counselors when such a request is made, a need is perceived, or if the subject is non-spiritual.

The pastor, trustees, and employees have fiduciary responsibilities to the church. This means that they are to act in the best interest of the church with diligence and according to the best ethical practices, laws, and regulations that guide the work of a non-for-profit organization. When they knowingly breach their fiduciary responsibilities and break the trust and confidence placed on them by the church and its members they could incur personal liabilities for their acts.

Personal Liabilities

The preceding comment on breach of fiduciary responsibilities and personal liabilities brings us to a wider discussion on clergy personal liabilities with regard to the Internal Revenue Service. The IRS requires churches and other organizations to deduct payroll withholding taxes and forward them to the government. But when accounting staff, pastor, or volunteer willfully fail to collect and pay the withholding taxes he or she will be personally liable to penalties:

> Section 6672(a) imposes a penalty against any person required to collect, truthfully account for, and pay over any tax imposed by the Code who willfully fails to collect, or truthfully account for and pay over the tax, or who willfully attempts in any manner to evade or defeat the tax.
>
> Under section 6671(b), the term "person" includes an officer or employee of a corporation or a member or employee of a partnership, who, as an officer, employee, or member of the corporation or partnership, is under a duty to perform the act in respect of which the violation occurs.[1]

The IRS will also have an axe to grind with a pastor, trustee, or finance committee member if transactions with certain key members of the church (such as the pastor, trustees, staff, and substantial contributors) are not done at arm's length and if there is an "excess benefit" to such member(s). Excess benefit transactions usually arise in cases of disposal of church assets, interest-free loans or write-off of loans, and salaries and allowances to key ("disqualified") persons of the church. The penalty for excess benefit could be the loss of the church's tax-exempt status and the sanctioning of the person engaged (the approving officer or benefiting member) in excess benefit transactions. This is how the IRS defines excess benefit:

> An excess benefit transaction is a transaction in which an economic benefit is provided by an applicable tax-exempt organization, directly or indirectly, to or for the use of a disqualified person, and the value of the economic benefit provided by the organization exceeds the value of the consideration received by the organization.
>
> To determine if an excess benefit transaction occurred, include all consideration and benefits exchanged between or among the disqualified person and the applicable tax-exempt organization and all entities it controls.
>
> In addition, if a supporting organization makes a grant, loan, payment of compensation, or similar payment to a substantial contributor of the organization, the arrangement is an excess benefit transaction. The entire amount of the payment is taxable as an excess benefit.
>
> In an excess benefit transaction, the general rule for the valuation of property, including the right to use property, is fair market value. Fair market value is the price at which property, or the right to use property, would change hands between a willing buyer and a willing seller, neither being under any compulsion to buy, sell,

---

1. Internal Revenue Service, "Internal Revenue Bulletin: 2005–24," Sec. 2: Background.

or transfer property or the right to use property, and both having reasonable knowledge of all relevant facts.

An excess benefit can occur in an exchange of compensation and other compensatory benefits in return for the services of a disqualified person, or in an exchange of property between a disqualified person and the applicable tax-exempt organization.[2]

One of the ways to avoid falling into "excess benefit transactions" is for the church to seek professional advice on the fair value of assets during sale, to put in place a rigorous conflict of interest policy, and a market-tested compensation package for clergy and employees.

Premises

A church is likely going to incur costs and penalties for injuries persons suffer on its premises. It is the duty of the pastor and board of trustees that the church environment is safe and secure and the church is covered with adequate liability insurance.

Commercial Contracts

Failure to fulfill the terms of a contract will likely result in penalties if disagreements are not settled amicably. More importantly, pastors and church officials who sign documents on behalf of their churches could be personally exposed in case of non-performance of contracts by their churches. So it is important for the signers of contracts to ensure that the church's bylaws allow for their indemnification. The corporate veil, however, could be lifted if it is discovered that the officer acted outside the laws of the church or her implied authority. What I mean is that if the pastor acts outside his or her authority as specified by the bylaws of the church, he or she will be personally held liable for such abuse of executive powers.

Political Campaigns

Engaging in political campaigns is considered an improper and illegal activity for churches with 501(c)(3) status of the Federal Internal Revenue Code. An organization with tax-exempt status is prohibited from "political

---

2. Internal Revenue Service, "Intermediate Sanctions—Excess Benefit Transactions."

lobbying or endorsing a candidate for public office" or attempting "to influence legislation as a substantial part of its activities." Tax-exempt organizations are also expected not to raise funds or donate funds for political candidates, distribute advertisement and campaign materials for political candidates, or participate in activities that are either beneficial or detrimental to a candidate. If the rules are violated the church could lose its tax-exempt status as a punishment.

The restriction that applies to participating in political campaigns does not mean that churches cannot inform their members about political issues or public debates in an election cycle and encourage them to register to vote.

Financial Matters

When we discussed the "Statement of Activities" earlier we stated that donors give funds under "restricted or unrestricted" categories. Restriction can be permanent or temporary. Part of the compliance process, the procedure for avoiding legal liabilities, or for potentially incurring the wrath of donors is to have a system of internal controls that ensures that funds are properly classified and that the conditions stipulated for each class of donations are strictly followed.

Another key point to remember is that as a tax-exempt corporation the earnings and assets of the church should not inure to private individuals or provide a substantial benefit to private interests:

> Churches and religious organizations, like all tax exempt organizations under IRC section 501(c)(3), are prohibited from engaging in activities that result in inurement of the church's or organization's income or assets to insiders (i.e., persons having personal and private interest in the activities of the organization). *Insiders* could include the minister, church board members, officers, and in certain circumstances, employees. Example of prohibited inurement include the payment of dividends, the payment of unreasonable compensation to insiders, and transferring property to insiders for less than fair market value. The prohibition against inurement is absolute; therefore, any amount of inurement is, potentially, grounds for loss of tax-exempt status. In addition the insider involved may be subject to excise tax.... Note that prohibited inurement does not include reasonable payments for services rendered, payments that

further tax-exempt purposes, or payments made for the fair market value of real or personal property.³

The third issue we want to discuss under "Financial Matters" is insurance. It is absolutely important for a parish or church to have adequate insurance for its assets and collections. In addition, there should be periodic auditing (usually annually) of the church books. An expert (from inside or external body) is to examine the financial records and accounting practices of the church, evaluate the adequacy of its internal control systems, and investigate the tax and compliance obligations of the church. The report of the expert or the auditing team should be submitted to the church board and management personnel that can take the necessary actions to correct anomalies.

The effort to institutionalize periodic audits should not be taken lightly. In recent times we have read reports of pastors stealing from the collection plates and also charging personal expenses to the churches' credit cards. One pastor in Connecticut stole over $1.4 million over many years. Conducting periodic audits is one way to detect fraud early and stamp it out. This is not to say that the main goal of audits is to detect frauds, instead it is to evaluate and render professional opinion on the overall quality of the accounting systems, records, financial statements, internal control systems, and compliance obligations.

Good Compliance and Good Practices

Compliance in accounting means recording, managing, and presenting the financial affairs and information of the church in accordance with federal, state, and municipal laws and regulations, and with the generally accepted accounting standards. At its core it means that the deployment and use of resources of the church are in line with the standards of regulating and supervising agencies and with the expectations of key constituencies of the church. There is something "religious" about compliance, especially when we examine it in the light of the etymology of religion. The word religion *(religio)* could be possibly traced to *religare*, meaning bond or binding. The demands of compliance bound the organization to certain rules and standards of practice. *Relegere* is also an etymon of religion and it refers to carefulness in the separation of spheres. Relegere, according to Giorgio Agamben:

3. Internal Revenue Service, *Tax Guide for Churches*, 5; italics in the original.

> Indicates the stance of scrupulousness and attention that must be adopted in relations with the gods, the uneasy hesitation (the "rereading [rileggere]"] before forms—and formulae—that must be observed in order to respect the separation between the sacred and the profane. *Religio* is not what unites men and gods but what ensures they remain distinct. It is not disbelief and indifference toward the divine, therefore, that stand in opposition to religion, but "negligence," that is, a behavior that is free and "distracted" (that is to say, released from the *religio* of norms) before things and their use, before forms of separation and their meaning.[4]

So in the matters of compliance the pastor is expected to firmly connect the church to the standards, principles, and regulations of governmental and professional oversight bodies, and also to treat with utmost carefulness the resources of God and human beings committed to her stewardship. Compliance points to the need for scrupulous observance of accounting-tax-managerial "ritual" practices in the leadership of the church. Compliance is an expression of her commitment to the sacred oath of safeguarding the assets and liabilities of the church and ordering relationship between the world of the church, its publics, and God. In a crude sense, failure to comply with the established standards or practices may be akin to profanation. In the light of relegere, "to profane, means to open the possibility of a special form of negligence, which ignores separation or, puts it to a particular use."[5] Compliance failure may also arise because of inappropriate use of resources of the church.

Insofar as a pastor, especially of a small church, can never be certain that she has met all the standards and expectations of her constituencies she is forever embedded in a logic of guilt, a guilt without once and for all redemption or atonement. Every year the demands of compliance are made new and thus her guilt is incessantly turned toward more guilt, more incompleteness. She can deliver herself from this anxiety if she seeks help from a competent attorney or accountant.

The accounting and legal issues that pertain to liabilities and compliance are often seen as only relating to managerial decision-making or corporate ethics, which is limited to avoiding financial risks. But we need to go beyond this restricted perspective. When this writer examined the accounting and legal issues as they relate to liabilities and compliance from the lens of philosophy a whole new world of understanding opened up. I

4. Agamben, *Profanation*, 74–75; italics in the original.
5. Ibid., 75.

began to grasp them as social practices with a specific ontology of personhood. The whole theory and practice of accounting is based on two basic ideas, which enable the profession to strive for "knowledge and truth" that come from a language that can code, formalize, and universalize the day-to-day operations of any entity.

The first premise is that the entity is an identifiable person with clearly distinguishable boundaries, a discrete and persisting entity. The person or organization is a purely, singly, and integrally whole entity for which a set of account can be kept. The second assumption is that input and output, credit and debit, the resources available for entity's use is exactly equal to the resources the owners and creditors have provided. The ironclad conviction about the balancing of the scales of justice or clear equalization inevitably denies that "there would be the graceful granting that comes from overfullness, of the excessive inexhaustible, and irreplaceable endowment of every being."[6]

These two paradigmatic principles constitute the *arche*, paving the way for the realization of its *telos*, which is a resolution of meaning, a defined naming of balance. With the two ideas and their concomitant arche and telos, accounting appears to me as a form of moral thought "animated by the belief in the possibility of a nonambivalent, non-aporetic ethical code."[7] This form of moral thought, better non-moral thought, is the common characteristic and predicament of not only accounting but also economics and politics as society has "drifted from *having* a market economy to *being* a market."[8] Philosopher Michael Sandel of Harvard University puts it well when he states:

> Our politics is overheated because it is mostly vacant, empty of moral and spiritual content. It fails to engage with big questions that people care about.
>
> The moral vacancy of contemporary politics has a number of sources. One is the attempt to banish notions of good life from public discourse. In the hopes of avoiding sectarian strife, we often insist that citizens leave their moral and spiritual convictions behind when they enter the public square. But despite its good intentions, the reluctance to admit arguments about the good life

---

6. Ulfers and Cohen, "Friedrich Nietzsche as Bridge," 4.

7. Bauman, *Postmodern Ethics*, 9, quoted in Ulfers and Cohen, "Friedrich Nietzsche as Bridge," 4.

8. Sandel, *What Money Can't Buy*, 10; italics in the original.

into politics prepared the way for market triumphalism and for the continuing hold of market reasoning.⁹

This way of looking at accounting opens up a vista to examine the philosophy of neoclassical economics and accounting and its possible relation to theology of money. With the idea of persons interacting, exchanging resources, and trying to meet the expectations of standards, excellences, and virtues compliance is a social phenomenon, indeed a social practice with a given "ontology of personhood" as defined by a monetary, market economy. In order to adequately understand accounting as expressed through compliance and to grasp money we must make a serious attempt to comprehend their underlying ontology of personhood. And to develop a theology of money, we must either side with the accounting-and-market-based ontology of personhood or develop an alternative vision.

Theology in Motion 7: Money and Personhood

The problem of money is the problem of creating and maintaining an embracing economic community (reciprocal relatedness). At the foundational level of every monetary/economic system or theory there is a conception of what a person is and an account of how persons are related to one another. This is not surprising because insofar as economics is a study of human activity there has to be some model of human behavior. Thusly, any systematic theological investigation of the modern monetary system that envisions to transform human patterns of interaction within the economic system must provide from the beginning a theory of personhood on which its vision is based.

This programmatic statement needs some clarification; we need to unpack it at six different levels of elucidation and depth. Each level provides a set of reasons why any Christian theology of money must start from an analysis of personhood. For this term is so full of implications for understanding modern society and money that it is pertinent to reflect on it as the unavoidable point of departure.

First, at the heart of current economists' understanding of money is the concept of personhood operative in economic science—the *homo economicus* ("*economic man*," a methodological construct of psychological atomism, egoism, and hedonism). In the neoclassical economic view

---

9. Ibid., 13–14.

of humans and human actions, which dominates contemporary monetary thinking, the existence of a human person is regarded as only individuated but not communally located for the simple reason of generating reliable predictions and explanations. The individual is abstracted from her social context in which her decisions are made and actions take place.

Economists have developed this model of humans which puts forth the economic agent as rational, only self-interested, and with perfect information. In maximizing her interest, relations and relationships are instrumental and not ends in themselves or are not constitutive of her self-definition. This model needs to be challenged and an alternative one developed which is open to the whole creative and ontological nature of humans without destroying the vitality and utility of the concept of the *economic man*.

Neoclassical economism does not require the individual to live a flourishing social life, nor even that she desires the good of her community. Rather it simply requires her to express her choice or preference rationally and match her means to her chosen values and ends. The way anyone can know her preference or is allowed to investigate her preference is to examine the way she votes with her money in the market. She is assumed to be a solitary, rational utility maximizer. She is *homo economicus*, quite similar to Martin Buber's "capricious man."[10] In this cold, neoclassical praxeological model of mainstream economists, social relations are depersonalized; indeed solid relations have melted into thin air and the world has been transformed into a chain of mathematical problems.

Neoclassical economics does not place much accent on understanding personhood (which is being plus being-in-relation) beyond mere broaching it as "transactors who are in a state of reciprocal independence."[11] But people are not monads, and thus theologians and ethicists who are serious about capturing the actual nature of personhood in their scholarship cannot just use the *homo economicus* concept of personhood in their theologizing about money. The economic and sociological foundations necessary for crafting a robust systematic theology of money cannot be fully set in place without a concept of personhood that is capable of countering the narrow neoclassical concept of "rational" autonomous *homo economicus*.

Second, if one understands personhood as being in communion, it has other implications for the way one theologizes about money. Like personhood, money also has its place, only in the community. As Otto A. Piper put it, "there is no private money. As a means of exchange, money has

---

10. Buber, *I and Thou*, 110.
11. Gregory, *Gifts and Commodities*, 12, quoted in Tanner, *Economy of Grace*, 50.

its place [only] within a community."[12] Money enables person-in-relation communion everywhere. This person-in-relation communion that money enables is received as well as given. It is a shared participation in which each economic agent contributes and others contribute to her. Because money is a social practice, as we have shown, the participation it creates through the giving and receiving is fully present only among all in the community. Behind every person with power to be in relationship is the "capacity or minimum personal qualification which those exercising the power" to be in communion with others must possess. Thus, a systematic theology of money needs to provide an analysis of capabilities that every person will need in order to fully participate and flourish in his or her community and contribute to its preservation and progress.

Third, all monetary thinking is ultimately philosophical and profoundly ethical. It seeks to fashion a way of regulating life, human interactions, and presents a regime that best controls the inevitable clash and conflicts among persons in a community. It aims either to preserve or profoundly change the characteristic form of a society. In one case it strives to avoid at best what is wrong or ugly about a regime. In the other, it seeks to gain a better form of interaction. Both claim to be grounded on some conception of what is the good. Thus, monetary economics is essentially political. And theology of money is essentially philosophical and ethical. It is a form of political thinking as it is directed to some purpose as its good.

Fourth, monetary thinking as a political thought cannot secure a strong footing without specifying the nature of human beings it considers as normative. Paul Tillich rightly said, "The roots of political thought must be sought in human being itself. Without some notion of human nature, of its powers and tensions, one cannot make any statements about the foundations of political science and thought. Without a doctrine of human nature, there can be no theory of political tendencies that is more than a depiction of their external form."[13]

Fifth, Christian theologians need to put forward a concept of personhood that will not silent the salient questions which need to be answered before they are posed. We need to come up with an understanding of personhood that can effectively address the existential ambiguities of money. One of such ambiguities is that money connects and disconnects, unifies and divides, embraces and excludes. We need a concept of personhood

---

12. Piper, "That Strange Thing Money," 219.
13. Tillich, *Socialist Decision*, 2.

that can counter the disconnecting tendencies of money—that is one that does not add to the centrifugal pull by presenting society as a collection of monads, unrelated, self-contained individuals, but rather does recognize the deep and total sociality of all forms of human existence.

Finally, we need to think of personhood in a way that can form the foundation of money and the global monetary system that are capable of drawing persons and nations more generally into a mutually participative life.[14] It is only appropriate that a form of anthropology be worked out now that informs not only our thinking on money, but also holds the possibility of more mutually participative economic life, capable of enabling us to ask questions about the moral and spiritual content of our economic life, and admit arguments about the good life into our economics.

This will be a relational ontology of personhood. It is an understanding of human beings as relational beings made in the image of God and not in the image of the market. This perspective has to be a dominant if not determinative factor for the crafting of a theology of money. "The social dimension of human life, the fact that human beings exist in specific societal relations to other human beings . . . [has to be] the dominant feature for any attempt at determining the structure and destiny of" our modern monetary system.[15]

Unlike the neoclassical economic concept of personhood, *homo economicus* with focus on independence, isolation, razor-edged competition, this relational personhood accents inclusiveness, mutuality, communion in modern economies where inequality, separation, and division are rampant. More importantly, relational personhood provides philosophical-theological basis for new forms of monetary system that can create, maintain, and enhance equitable patterns of interrelatedness and genuine universal community. This conception of personhood prepares the ground to apply the "ethics" of trinitarian communion (*imago Dei*) to the architecture of our financial systems and how to nudge national monetary systems or financial communities to align with God's community.

The problem of money is the problem of creating and maintaining an embracing economic community.[16] We need a theology of money and

14. Cunningham, "Participation as Trinitarian Virtue," 18.

15. Schwöbel, "Human Being as Relational Being," in Schwöbel and Gunton, *Persons, Divine and Human*, 142.

16. This is also the task of the late American philosopher Josiah Royce, who in 1913 set before Christians and all human endeavors: the creation of genuine universal community. "But what I mean is that since the office of religion is to aim towards the creation

monetary systems that draw on the perichoretic understanding of the Trinity, which holds the tension between the one and many at balance, will liberate the monetary system from the vise-grip of exclusion, and deliver it into marvelous embrace of reciprocal relatedness. "In an embrace the identity of the self is both preserved and transformed, and the alterity of the other is both affirmed as alterity and partly received into the ever changing identity of the self."[17] This is the real good news that we can bring to bear upon the challenges of the contemporary monetary system.

In chapter 10 we will lay out the kind of monetary policy that can create and maintain an embracing economic community. But before we reach there as the culmination of our study of accounting and money, we need to do some *bush clearing* so that the light of analysis in chapter 10 will shine brighter and its persuasive power enhanced. First, in chapter 8, we will show that theological ideas have for centuries undergirded the operations of the global monetary and financial systems. This historical perspective is necessary to show that subjecting economic systems to theological critique and crafting theological-ethical principles to inform their operations is not the invention of this study. This writer is only following a tradition well worth preserving.

In chapter 9, I offer an elaborate theological critique of accounting, the fundamental accounting equation. The critique is designed to do two things. First, it will deepen the student's understanding of the fundamental accounting equation. Second, the subtle analyses of the chapter will show that accounting carries heavy theological-philosophical freight. The equation is not merely a mathematical expression but a neat and discerning summation of a worldview, a perspective of human relations that does not always fit with the biblical view of human sociality.

---

on earth of the Beloved [Universal] Community, the future task of religion is the task of inventing and applying the arts which shall win men over to unity, and which shall overcome their original hatefulness by the gracious love, not of mere individuals, but of communities. Now such arts are still to be discovered. Judge every social device, every proposed reform, every national and every local enterprise by the one test: Does this help towards the coming of the universal community." Royce, *Problem of Christianity*, 404–5; italics in the original.

17. Volf, *Exclusion and Embrace*, 143.

Exercises

1. Explain the compliance burden as it relates to churches with 501(c)(3) status.
2. What is the difference between IRS forms I-9 and W-9?
3. Discuss excess benefit transactions as it relates to churches.
4. Discuss and evaluate the neoclassical economics conception of personhood.
5. What is the arche and telos of accounting? What are their implications for a theological or Christian understanding of the collective economic life?

CHAPTER 8

The Moral Roots of the Global Financial Industry

Introduction

TODAY, THE EXTENT TO which a Judeo-Christian ethos and ethics stand behind the global financial system is not widely recognized. Modern financial thought believes itself to have autonomous existence from religious thought and theology, and to be determined only by the laws of reason and market. But this is an inaccurate reading of the intellectual history of the global financial system. The Judeo-Christian heritage of the Western world helped to create the modern financial system and established the intellectual framework whereby the ethos that now shape the modern global financial system came into being. The formation of the system was suffused with theological and moral insights which are currently being reworked, relatively actualized, and recast in a new language but not totally forsaken. The rootedness of the global financial system in the Judeo-Christian ethos today is not revealed in the subjection of secular financial dealings to ecclesiastical or explicit biblical laws, but by a common commitment to moral principles anchored to the Judeo-Christian heritage.

This chapter unveils the hidden religious assumptions behind the financial dimension of economic ideas and practices and points to the rationalizing impetus that contributed toward the creation of technical tools and systems underlying the production and distribution of credit in the global trade and payment system. The thesis is that Christian theology and practices influenced the development of the global financial industry by enhancing certain economic and ideational possibilities conducive for its emergence and growth. This is a thesis that has been argued for the whole capitalist system by Rodney Stark.[1] In this chapter I am particularly extending his reasoning into the global financial industry. I will show more clearly the way that Christian theology and faith in progress translated into technical and organizational innovations and informed economic philosophy and practice in the financial industry. The examples and the numerous suggestive clues I have assembled from a variety of historical sources are to be seen as an invitation to sustained historical research and as an emerging hypothesis rather than a finished and exhaustive argument. Their main purpose is to point to further research into the historical connection between morality and the global financial system as well as to stimulate further investigation of the religious and moral bases of the ideational, economic, and technological changes that transformed the ethos of the modern financial system.

My discussion is organized under three major headings: (1) value-foundations of the economy, (2) ethos of the financial market, and (3) summary and concluding thoughts. In the first section, I discuss the general values that underlie the economic system within which financial corporations operate. The second section takes a look at the specific values that are foundational to the working of the financial system. Finally, I provide a summary of my findings and offer some concluding thoughts. The overarching conclusion is that, for the most part, the moral core of modern financial thinking proceeded from Judeo-Christian theological thought. The major and foundational concepts of financial economics are secularized versions of religious concepts, and if we intend to revitalize, critique, reform, or reconstruct the monetary system in our global environment we shall have to consciously wrestle with the morality and value system of its actors.

Value-Foundations of the Economy

In this section, I discuss the general value system that undergirds the economic system within which financial corporations operate. In this regard, my analysis focuses on five areas: property rights, individualism, the invisible hand of the market, production of trust, and work ethic.

1. Stark, *Victory of Reason*.

Accounting and Money for Ministerial Leadership

Respect for Property Rights

In a sense the financial system is about the trading of property rights over money or securities that entail claims over assets. The Judeo-Christian respect for and encouragement of property rights were very crucial in the sustenance of the international financial system in its early days, especially after the fall of the Roman Empire, which had protected property rights. The Roman Catholic Church became the most important society-wide institution in the western territory of the defunct empire. Since biblical times, there has been some kind of sanctity of possessions. The Ten Commandments prohibit stealing and even coveting what belongs to someone else. We hear Moses, when his leadership was challenged, saying, "I have not taken one ass from them, nor have I wronged any of them" (Num 16:15). The prophet Samuel also echoed the same feeling when the Israelites asked for a king (1 Sam 12:3). In addition, biblical teachings contain prophetic rebukes for abuse of power by earthly rulers and deliver constant reminders that all powers and wealth belong to God—those having political power and economic wealth only hold them in trust for God. In consideration of these teachings in western medieval Christianity, David Landes argues that they "implicitly gave protection to private property. . . . Earthly rulers were not free to do as they pleased, and even the Church, God's surrogate on earth, could not flout rights and take at will. The elaborate paperwork that accompanied the transfer of gifts of the faithful bore witness to the duty of good practice and proper procedure."[2] Property rights protected the dignity of persons and the integrity of families. In fact, in his masterly book *The Wealth and Poverty of Nations*, Landes argues that Europe leapt ahead of other societies like China, which in the Middle Age was ahead of the West, because of its Judeo-Christian ethic that China did not have. In other words, ethos matters in economic development.

Individualism

The biblical emphasis on egalitarianism and equal dignity for all human beings is very important in understanding the ethos that lies behind the financial market as it developed in the West. Unlike other parts of the ancient world, which gave dignity to only some and not all, the biblical notion of every human being created in the image of God provided a powerful drive

---

2. Landes, *Wealth and Poverty of Nations*, 35.

not only toward individualism, but also for fashioning social structures that would respect the equal dignity of all. In fact, Jonathan Sacks, the Chief Rabbi of Great Britain, enthuses that the most influential single phrase in Western civilization is Genesis 1:26: "Let us make man in our image and likeness." Because each person carries the image of God, the central question, according to Sacks, is: "How do we build social structures that honor and sustain the freedom, integrity and creativity of the individual?"[3] It is a long road in the development of individualism from the Bible to the present. This chapter will not trace the map of the road; noting two landmarks along the road will suffice.

First, the French anthropologist and catholic scholar Louis Dumont has argued that the modern individualism that dominates various aspects of Western culture has its roots in Christianity, with its unrelenting emphasis on the individual as the sole unit of divine judgment. Only individuals are objects of salvation, not families, churches, towns, or nations. The individual, "an independent, autonomous, and thus essentially nonsocial moral being," that carries the paramount value of society is principally of Judeo-Christian heritage.[4] The development of modern individualism moved in two steps. This emphasis enabled individuals to step out of their traditional social world and paved the way for individualism to develop.

Second, the individualism that emerged—especially after the Reformation—was conducive to business as it placed a high premium on individual life and moral behavior in the spheres of the family, work, church, and public. The Calvinist strand of the Reformation considered both material progress and religious and moral improvement as desirable because worldly success was either an indication of divine favor or an outward sign of inward grace. According to Benjamin M. Friedman, Harvard economist, John Calvin and his followers:

> Aspired to carry human society to new heights not just by reforming the church and the institutions of the state, but also through their individual conduct and example. While the English Puritans and their spiritual descendants saw secular progress as inevitable, at the same time human effort directed toward bringing that progress about was a moral imperative.... The Puritan "saints," as they called themselves, took it as their collective duty to reform society

---

3. Sacks, *Dignity of Difference*, 92.
4. Dumont, *Essays on Individualism*, 25.

and thereby create the new Christian Commonwealth. And they also strived individually to achieve material prosperity.[5]

The Invisible Hand of the Market

Adam Smith's notion of the invisible hand is at the heart of modern understanding of the market. "It is not from the benevolence of the butcher, the brewer, or the baker that we expect our dinner, but from their regard to their own interest. We address ourselves, not to their humanity but to their self love."[6] He is deservedly famous for the phrase, "invisible hand" with respect to the market in *The Wealth of Nations* (1776). What is rarely recognized is the origin of this idea, which is traceable to John Calvin and Saint Augustine of Hippo. Unlike many scholars, I trace the source of the idea of the invisible hand to both Calvin and Augustine rather than to Calvin alone. What many have not acknowledged is that there are two grand ideas in the image of the invisible hand. There is the idea of a kind of "providence" and self-organization that is traceable to Calvin. And there is the other idea of harnessing and transforming passions and vices into something constructive that works toward the general welfare, which, according to Albert O. Hirschman, is traceable to Augustine.

Calvin had written about God's providence sustaining order in the world and referred to it as an invisible hand. Smith translated this image into economic language.[7] Instead of the world being organized by God, an external agent imposing order from without, Smith reasoned that the market is self-organizing because of an automatic harmony in the relationship between agents in the market. For Smith, order grows from within, endogenous and spontaneous. Each human actor pursuing her own interest serves the public good. This is not the only way Smith developed his economic version of the divine providence. "Just as traditional Calvinist theology distinguishes general and special providence, so Smith draws a distinction between the *general* tendency toward [market] equilibrium and

---

5. Friedman, *Moral Consequences*, 42.

6. Smith, *Wealth of Nations*, 15.

7. For a discussion of Smith's Calvinist leanings, see R. Nelson, *Reaching for Heaven*, 278–90; R. Nelson, *Economics as Religion*, 95–106.

special cases of equilibrium. The overall framework Smith established continues to set the terms for much of analysis today."[8]

Smith appropriated Calvin's idea first through aesthetics. He had used the image of the invisible hand in his *The Theory of Moral Sentiments* (1759). In the section "Of the beauty which the appearance of UTILITY bestows upon all production of art, and the extensive influence of this species of Beauty," he wrote:

> They are led by an invisible hand to make nearly the same distribution of the necessaries of life, which would have made, had the earth been divided into equal portions among all its inhabitants, and thus without intending it, without knowing it, advance the interest of the society, and afford the means to the multiplication of the species. When Providence divided the earth among few lordly masters, it neither forgot nor abandoned those seemed to have been left out in the partition. . . . The same principle, the love of system, the same regard to beauty of order, of art and contrivance, frequently serves to recommend those institutions which tend to promote the public welfare.[9]

Recently, Lisa Hill has joined a rising chorus of scholarly voices to argue that the image of the invisible hand not only has a theological origin but expresses a hidden theology of Smith. Anthony Waterman in 2002 put forward the suggestion that Smith could be read as offering a kind of Augustinian theodicy of the market. According to him, Smith's idea could be interpreted as thus: just like God put governments in place to restrain sin, the institution of the market also restrains sin.[10]

Albert Hirschman traces the origin of the image of the invisible hand to Saint Augustine. The fourth-century theologian cautiously spoke of the possibility of using one vice to check another—the desire for wealth could be suppressed by the desire for glory or the love of praise. In the hands of later writers, cautiousness was thrown overboard and the love of glory was purported to have "redeeming social value." It was in this appropriation and adaptation of Augustine's idea that the image of the invisible hand emerged in medieval times. Hirschman writes:

---

8. Taylor, *Confidence Games*, 239.

9. Smith, *Moral Sentiments*, 185, quoted in Taylor, *Confidence Games*, 85.

10. See Hill, "Hidden Theology," 1–29; Alvey, "Lisa Hill's Discovery"; Waterman, "Economics as Theology," 673–86; Waterman, *Political Economy*; Oslington, "Natural Theology."

Accounting and Money for Ministerial Leadership

> In fact, the idea of an "Invisible Hand"—of a force that makes men pursuing their private passions conspire unknowingly toward the public good—was formulated in connection with the search for glory, rather than with the desire for money, by Montesquieu. The pursuit of honor in monarchy, so he says, "brings life to all the parts of the body politic"; as a result, "it turns out that everyone contributes to the general welfare while thinking that he works for his own interests.[11]

Hirschman noted too that Blaise Pascal and some of his Jansenist contemporaries also anticipated Smith. They argued that self-love in spite of being sinful is workable and can hold society together better than charity.[12]

Other theories of the market were developed as medieval theologians sought to understand the process of price formation in the market. The debater of Martin Luther over papal authority, Thomas De Vio, Cardinal Cajetan (1468–1534), in his 1499 treatise (*De Cambiis*) sought to explain the foreign exchange market from a moral point of view. In the process, he developed the idea that the value of money could be affected by expectations about the future state of the market, thus anticipating by nearly five hundred years the twentieth-century expectation theory in economics.[13] Other medieval scholastics like Pierre de Jean Olivi, Luis Saravia, Cardinal Juan de Lugo, and Luis de Molina also developed various ideas about the working of the price system. They hit on the modern idea that value depends on subjective valuation of individuals and not on objective factors like the cost of production.[14]

Production of Trust

The economy and its operation cannot be adequately understood without trust and the shared ethos that underlie it. In this subsection I discuss how businesspersons, and especially bankers, have used trust to solve technical problems of trade and investment. Then I put forward the role played by Judeo-Christian heritage in creating the shared ethical norms that make the production of trust possible in the first place.

---

11. Hirschman, *Passions and the Interest*, 10.
12. Ibid., 17–56.
13. Woods, *How the Catholic Church*, 157–58.
14. Ibid., 158–60.

Many economists have given short shrift to trust, neglecting culture in their belief that the competitive market only considers revealed preferences encoded in price, supply, and demand data. But here I discuss the phenomenon of trust as it relates to the profit and loss considerations of any business enterprise. Trust is an institutionalized behavioral expectation based on sharing the same ethics and doing business by the same honest rules of the game. In an environment where the businessperson cannot get perfect information about a potential partner, and present and past performances cannot guarantee future performance, it becomes readily obvious that trust is necessary if anyone is to economize on transaction costs.[15] A business community minimizes transaction costs or opportunism by establishing ethics and codes of behavior that produce and maintain trust between people with commonly shared norms. Trust helps to keep the market in existence—without it transaction costs would be so high as to make exchange impossible. When a businessperson wants to choose her business partners, clients, suppliers, and valued customers, she will choose those she can trust because a greater degree of trust lowers the transaction costs of protecting contracts and sustaining relationships. In the financial industry it is always the general expectation that economic transaction should be secured by a more-than-economic relationship.

One cannot ignore the roles of religious and moral sanctions and religious network supporting contractual relations in the production of those trustworthy institutions, habits, and patterns that foment trust. Christianity and symbols of Christian identity have been and are used in many business circles to facilitate economic interactions and sometimes to exclude "outsiders" from participation in the "morality community" of the Christian network. Francis Fukuyama and Max Weber (in his less-known essay, "The Protestant Sects and the Spirit of Capitalism") have drawn attention to the role of Judeo-Christian heritage in producing certain cultural norms or shared ethics that promoted community and trust that encouraged economic exchange.[16] British sociologist Steve Bruce, remarking on trust, asceticism, piety, and work ethic of Protestant Quakers, observed: "It is not an accident that almost the entire British banking system developed from family firms run by Quakers: The Barclays, Backhouses, Trittons and Gurneys. If you had to ask someone to look after your money, ask a Quaker."[17]

15. See Williamson, *Economic Institutions of Capitalism*.
16. Fukuyama, *Trust*.
17. Bruce, *God is Dead*, 23.

Accounting and Money for Ministerial Leadership

Work Ethic

Often analysts of the workings of the global financial system focus on its sophisticated financial products and its capability in directing investable resources from surplus areas to deficit areas while they ignore the work ethic beneath it all. Work ethic, or perhaps what has been termed the "Protestant work ethic," pervades and permeates all aspects of lives in the industry. The ethos of Wall Street is not only defined by profit drive but also by work ethic. The global industry is very much defined by work, its organization and schedules, sequence and temporal discipline, industriousness and desire to avoid waste of time. Bankers are busy and constantly on the move to do more work in shorter and shorter periods by using technology. One of the marks of responsibility is being able to finish one's work ahead of the time it is needed. When I worked on Wall Street the joke was that if your boss wanted something to be completed today, it meant he or she wanted it yesterday.

The idea of work is both an ethical and "theological" matter on Wall Street. Men and women are busy working to create their own conception of *eudaimonia*, which is survival of the organization plus personal survival, happiness, and progress. It is theological because work reflects a certain orientation toward the world that gives meaning to them, defining the purpose of their existence, shaping their perception of the interpersonal relationships that surround them, and enabling them to participate in something that is bigger than themselves. Money serves, for many people in the industry, as the ultimate indication of how this meaning and purpose have been successfully actualized. For such persons money affirms them as participants in the creative development of humankind.

The above view no doubt contains elements of ethics and theology, but does not account for deeper meaning of work that is present in the whole Western culture—or even in the industry itself. Other dimensions of the ethos of the modern work ethic of the financial corporation indicate that ethic and structure of work are deeply rooted in the religious dynamics of life. Max Weber, in his *The Protestant Ethic and the Spirit of Capitalism*, drew attention to the power of religion in the forming of the work ethic that undergirds capitalism. Under the social teachings of the Church, work was seen as a form of civic virtue, a contribution to the good of God's creation, and a means of working out one's *calling* in the "theater of glory." From Pope Leo XIII's encyclical *Rerum Novarum* (1891), to Pope John Paul II's *Laborem Excerens* (1981), the Roman Catholic Church has defined and redefined philosophy and social questions of human work so as to lay out a Christian perspective on work. The writings of Luther and other Reformed theologians on calling see an intrinsic value in the works that Christians do and elevate such work to the level of a service to God. Luther extended the meaning of vocation from being a particular kind of religious life to every type of work—raising work in all sectors of society to the level of a divine service. Yale University's Miroslav Volf comments that Luther's approach to human work ascribed greater value to work than was previously the case and overcame the medieval subordination of *vita activa* to the *vita contemplativa*. "Since every vocation rests on God's commission, every vocation is fundamentally of the same value before God."[18]

It is important to note that when we are describing the work ethic of the people on Wall Street or in the London financial district we are not just talking about personality traits, or about getting up early in the morning and going to work and putting in a hard day's work. Subsistence farmers may do that. Work ethic is here broadly defined. It is as Francis Fukuyama argues, the whole of creative concern about modern wealth generation and associated pursuit of "technology, innovation, organization, and a host of other factors related to the quality rather than the simple quantity of labor used to create it . . . a rational approach to problem solving . . . that inclines individuals to master their environment through innovation and labor."[19] This ethic as Fukuyama, following Weber, has argued rests on deeply rooted Protestant values and presuppositions and doctrines of calling and covenant.

Ethos of the Financial Market

In the larger context of an ethos that stresses property rights, individualism, providential development, trust, and a work ethic, we can focus more closely on the ethos of the financial system. One starting point for investigating such specific ethos is to examine a culture in three areas: time, risk, and risk diversification. Time and risk are the dominant factors in any financial decision model. Decisions makers are also interested in how to manage the risks that ensue from their decisions. What is the attitude toward time and risk or the philosophy that informs their understanding in that culture? A culture's understanding of time will condition the way its members define and act in the present toward planning and preparing for the future.

18. Volf, *Work in the Spirit*, 106.
19. Fukuyama, *Trust*, 45.

Accounting and Money for Ministerial Leadership

Attitudes Toward Time

Every financial decision made or product created to manage risk is a bet on time. Probability calculations that inform an investor's decisions are usually based on forecast of conditions that will prevail in the future. For instance, if an individual bets on winning a stake if heads comes up in one of ten tosses of a perfect coin, she is really hoping that the short run will look like the long run. This is so because even when the best probability theory tells her that the chances of heads or tails are equal at 50 percent, there is no guarantee that a head will show up in the first ten tosses. The chance of 50 percent is really for the long run. The managers of insurance companies are also betting on time:

> They set their premium to cover losses they will sustain in the long run; but when earthquakes and fires and hurricanes all happen about the same time, the short run can be very painful. . . . Risk and time are the opposite sides of the same coin, for if there is no tomorrow there would be no risk. Time transforms risk, and the nature of risk is shaped by the time horizon: the future is the playing field.[20]

The spread of Christianity in Europe brought a change to the perception of time. The future was still a mystery as before, but now it was in the hands of God. It is not in the hands of "the Fates," as Greeks and Romans had them. Nor is it, "eat, drink, and be merry, for tomorrow you shall die." Time became a subject for moral behavior and faith. As Christians had faith in the future, contemplating a future that was no longer inscrutable, no longer in the hands of cruel impersonal forces, and with a hope for an afterlife with the God that holds the future, the present became an active playing field to prepare for the important future. Decisions had to be made over a widened time horizon. Economist Peter Bernstein argues that the "concept of thrift and abstinence that characterize the Protestant ethic evidenced the growing importance of the future relative to the present."[21]

It was not only in this way that Christianity changed the social psychology of time. Time was no longer seen as a master or some instrument of a deity, but the medium within which men and women work and order work and leisure. Instead of calculating and following the seasons and the

---

20. Bernstein, *Against the Gods*, 15.
21. Ibid., 21.

triangular powers of the sun, moon, and stars so that human rhythms could be adjusted to fit into them, the idea evolved into how human beings can:

> All the better control nature and transcend the cosmic forces in action for spiritual and moral reasons. . . . The idea that the efficient use of time is an ethical and theological matter and thus decisive in the basic pattern of the good life had to be developed. . . . It reflects a certain orientation toward meaning, God and the world. Such a notion is important only where people believe that the timeless and eternal is in some basic way related to the proximate, the temporal, and transient, and that we humans ought to, therefore, order the latter for the sake of the former.[22]

David Landes, in his book *Revolution in Time*, states that the development of time technology in Christian Europe was an attempt to triumph over human fallenness and not to align social life with some cosmological event and temporal discipline. All of this had theological grounding which has been lost to many in the financial industry as the focus is now only on the economic advantage of temporal discipline and the speed of business.[23]

Our discussion of time and its importance in the financial system would be incomplete without taking a look at time preference rate. Economics concerns itself with the mechanics of the inter-temporal flows of goods and services within and between societies. How this allocation for present and future satisfaction is done in any one society depends on the social rate of time preference of that society. Time preference is the rate at which society is willing to exchange consumption now for consumption tomorrow. It is the rate at which society is ready to transform the present into the future—and this is a deeply moral decision. What a society saves for its future out of its present resources, and therefore what it sets aside for investment, is primarily determined by the rate at which that society is willing to trade consumption now for consumption in the future. This decision about savings rate is a function of the dominant worldview and ethos as well as income, life expectancy, technology, and other socioeconomic factors.[24]

Time preference is a very important background concept in the financial industry. For instance, the valuation of financial products and even the payment of interest are based on this concept. In normal market conditions, ten-year bonds will carry a higher coupon rate than a one-year bond.

---

22. Stackhouse, "Moral Roots," 34.
23. Landes, *Revolution in Time*, 58–78.
24. See Sharp, *Economics of Time*, chap. 7; Lind, "Primer on the Major Issues," 21–114.

Also the value of a stream of cash two-years removed is worth less than the stream that is one-year removed from today.

Theological discussions in the medieval time had begun to focus on this concept. In his analysis, the scholastic theologian Martin de Azpilcueta (1493–1586) stated that "a claim on something is worth less than the thing itself, and . . . it is plain that that which is not useable for a year is less valuable than something of the same quality which is usable at once."[25] Earlier in 1285, a student of Saint Thomas Aquinas, Giles Lessines, had seen a connection between the idea of time preference and justice. According to him, "future goods are not valued so highly as the same goods available at an immediate moment of time, nor do they allow their owners to achieve the same utility. For this reason, it must be considered that they have a more reduced value in accordance with justice."[26] It is important to mention that this idea of time preference, important as it is known to be today, was not known well enough in medieval times to greatly influence the direction of the debate on usury, but it is an idea that later became useful in understanding price formation and the morality of interest charges in the marketplace. If it had been adequately known it would have taken some of the edge off the usury debate. Apart from any other consideration, interest is payable because of time preference. The loan that is given today is not of the same value as the one that will be received in the future. Interest, at the minimum, equalizes them.

These are not all the ways financial thought has proceeded from theology or in which the two are related. Both theology and financial thought have deep-seated eschatological orientations. Money—value of assets and liabilities—is always "eschatological in its structuring," that is, "the present is created from the future."[27] The value of assets or liabilities in the market system depends on anticipated flows of income, anticipated returns, promises of expansion in an imagined better future. Asset allocation decisions (deployment or withdrawal from the market) are always based on projections about value and income flows from assets in the future. Yet when this imagined future arrives, the value of the asset will still be based on expectations of what it will be in a further imagined future. Capital is trapped in a web of eschatological expectation of a better future—a being that is

---

25. Woods, *Church and the Market*, 117.

26. Ibid.

27. The nature appears akin to life as conceived by Gunton, *Father, Son and Holy Spirit*, 134–37, quote p. 136. See also Pannenberg, "God of Hope," 234–49, especially 243.

eternally becoming. As the British theologian Philip Goodchild aptly observed: "Capital is not merely a flow because it is always an anticipation of an imagined future—whether we are concerned with speculation or credit, it is always an anticipated rate of return that determines how much there will be. What there is now is dependent upon what we believe there will be: our eschatology determines our mode of being."[28]

Attitudes Toward Risk

Social and religious models and concepts shape how a people orient themselves meaningfully to uncertainty in everyday life. Risk is not some objective fact that can be discerned scientifically without the aid of ethos analysis. This is so because the content of risk is always interpreted by somebody or for somebody that is contextually situated and this exercise involves negotiating both natural and cultural, objective and subjective, boundaries. Hurricanes objectively exist in the Atlantic Ocean, but only become a risk for people who may potentially lose their lives if they are out in the open ocean or in its path. As Niels Henrik Gregersen has argued, every risk involves a semiotic triangle: (1) natural events, such as hurricanes, constitute the natural substrate of risk; (2) social events, such as our habits of conduct and expectation for the future, constitute the social definition of risk; and (3) the various meanings this socio-natural life holds for us is about the relevance and meaning of risk. "A risk is always a danger *of* something (sometimes natural, sometimes social) *for* somebody in a given nexus."[29]

It is from this phenomenological perspective that we can evaluate the roots of the risk-taking attitude on Wall Street. What is the role of the Christian social teachings in the development of the risk-willing predisposition? This involves asking questions about how Christianity encourages its adherents to accept potential losses with the expectation of overall positive outcome. This, according to Gregersen, could be done by any religion that positively values contingency and acknowledges risk in response to uncertainty.[30] Unlike the Greek notions of eternal world and fate, Christianity holds that the world is a contingent order created by God. In this sense both the existence of the world (its *existentia*) and its beautiful structure and quality (its *essentia*) are contingent. It also avers that the gift and

28. Goodchild, "Capital and Kingdom," 24–25.
29. Gregersen, "Risk and Religion," 356.
30. Ibid., 367.

the power to appreciate the world by humans are also contingent.[31] Thus both exterior (the world "out there") and interior gifts of the world depend on God.[32] Christianity, according to Gregersen who is working from the ideas of the German social philosopher Niklas Luhmann, identifies three forms of contingency:

> The fundamental contingency in Christian doctrine is the positive gift of existence, to which the risk of ultimate perdition is related. Second is the gift of the nontrivial qualities of life, to which the risks of trivialization and homogenization correspond. Third is the gift of being enabled to see and appreciate the beauty of the world, to which the risks of dullness and ingratitude correspond.[33]

In less technical language, Christianity encourages risk taking at the level of ordinary awareness. The parable of the ten talents related in Matthew 25:14–30 and Luke 19:11–27 puts a positive accent on human risk taking. The attitude of the servant who opted for a strategy of safety instead of taking risk for potential gain was condemned. In another place we are told, "I tell you the truth, unless a kernel of wheat falls to the ground and dies, it remains only a single seed. But if it dies, it produces many seeds" (John 12:24). Gregersen argues that the fundamental understanding of risk taking flows from a concept of God who has provided a habitable framework for risk taking. The world is controlled by a benevolent God who is not erratic, and risk undertaking in such a world is not a zero-sum game. The benefits of risk taking are greater than the potential damages.[34] Gregersen goes further even to argue that trinitarian theology can understand God as a risk-taking God.[35] He argues that the rational, reasonable God of the Christian faith is also a risk-taking God. He takes risk to love humankind, exposing himself to possible rejection, negligence, or risk of being misunderstood, and "by creating a world endowed with freedom."[36]

---

31. "'Contingency' means that which is neither necessary nor impossible, but *is* exactly because the loving God finds pleasure in the existence of such a world." Gregersen, "Faith in a World," 214–33.

32. The interior gifts refer to faith, hope, and love without which our ability to appreciate the world will be diminished.

33. Gregersen, "Risk and Religion," 367.

34. Ibid., 368.

35. Gregersen, "Faith in a World," 214–33.

36. Gregersen, "Risk and Religion," 355–76; quotes pp. 369–74.

This idea of a rational, reasonable God who created a habitable world that is rational and orderly, endowed with consistent physical laws, has led Christians into quantitative inquiry interested in how the rational universe works and has also promoted the emergence of products to protect against uncertainty. The conceptual frameworks engendered by these fundamental ideas are also indispensable in our understanding of the emergence of scientific thought.[37]

Managing the future does not stop at a society having a positive attitude toward risk. It is also about calculating and assessing risk exposure endemic in the future. This involves, among other efforts, calculations of probabilities and comprehending the law of probability. Understanding the law of probability was seen by some Christians in the medieval period as a moral issue.[38]

Risk Management Products

Future contracts and options generate turnover of billions of dollars in the global financial system. They are financially engineered products to manage risks. The historically uninformed observer may be fooled into thinking that because they are enormously sophisticated they are twentieth-century inventions. They are not. Aristotle in the fourth century before Christ wrote about one Thales of Melitus, who bought call options on oil presses. Thales was resentful of people saying that philosophy was useless and that it had left him poor, so he wanted to show naysayers that the subject was a worthwhile endeavor. He went on to profit from his knowledge of options. Aristotle explains:

> According to the story, he knew by his skill in the stars while it was still yet winter that there would be great harvest of olives in the coming year; so, having a little money, he gave deposits for use of all the olive-presses in Chios and Miletus, which he hired at a low price because no one bid against him. When the harvest-time came, and many were wanted all at once and of a sudden, he let them out at any rate which he pleased, and made a quantity of money.[39]

---

37. Woods, *How the Catholic Church*, 75–77.
38. Bernstein, *Against the Gods*, 43, 67.
39. Aristotle, *Politics*, 1259a10–16.

Closer to our own time, Christian monasteries were involved in the development of risk management products and used them to organize their finances.[40] For example, the Cistercian monks of medieval Europe copiously used futures in their business transactions. The Cistercians who had a reputation for the production of quality wools experimented with advance contracts with wool exporters. Their monasteries entered into multi-year future contracts with exporters. In this way, like the modern American farmer, they received cash advances in exchange for wools yet to be produced—the promised wool serving as security for the cash advances.[41] It was not only in financial risk management that the monasteries were involved. They also acted as credit establishments providing lending services for merchants as well providing safe havens for traveling merchants. The Church as a whole "proclaimed the wise doctrine of stable coinage," created systems of deposits, credit, and banking.[42]

In later Protestant history, churches in America played a crucial role in changing public perception about life-insurance investment/risk-management products. Turning around from an initial opposition to life insurance products because they thought it betrayed a lack of trust in God's providence, the churches in the eighteenth and nineteenth centuries were instrumental in creating the norm of personal financial responsibility toward survivors that was so necessary for the sustenance of the market, as Princeton University economic sociologist Viviana Zelizer points out. Christian religious leaders such as Reverend Henry Ward Beecher used their pulpits and sermons to encourage Christian men to make adequate provisions for dependents by buying life insurance. Beecher pointed out, "Once the question was: can a Christian man rightfully seek Life Assurance? That day is passed. Now the question is: can a Christian man justify himself in neglecting such a duty."[43]

40. Some economists have also seen connection between theological ideas developed in the medieval period and bankruptcy, a major modern risk management process in the modern economy. Bankruptcy lowers the cost to entrepreneurs in difficulties and gives them a second chance. The businessperson is given another chance to redeem herself commercially. This idea bears close analogy to the idea of purgatory in the medieval church. As Robert B. Ekelund et al puts it, purgatory represented the expiation of sins, a forgiveness of earthly transgressions that readied the soul for entry into heaven. Bankruptcy (instead of outright liquidation) like purgatory gives hope and has release time. See Ekelund et al, *Sacred Trust*, 154–55.

41. Ekelund et al, *Sacred Trust*, 52.

42. Ibid., 175.

43. Zelizer, "Human Values and the Market," 601–2.

The Moral Roots of the Global Financial Industry

While life insurance is a product to manage the risk survivors are exposed to after the death of the main breadwinner in the family, actuarial science forms the basis of calculating premiums for life insurance and annuities. Reverend Richard Price of England, a friend of America's Benjamin Franklin, is noted to have developed the mortality tables on which to base premiums. This made him the founding father of actuarial science.[44]

This example represents a whole set of techniques of managing risk that are broadly categorized by industry experts as "decision theory." Experts readily agree that deciding what to do in the face of uncertainty or probable outcomes is the first step in risk management. This field of finance and management (known as decision theory) is said to have begun with works of three theologians-ministers: Blaise Pascal, Antoine Arnauld, and Thomas Bayes. Pascal's 1660s wager, which asks, "God is, or he is not. Which way should we incline? Reason cannot answer"—started it all. Pascal framed the question of belief in God in line with the probable outcomes of a game of chance. In situations when decision makers cannot conduct experiments or rely on past experience, how should they make decisions in the face of outcomes that are different? The only way is to explore future consequences and then make a choice based on the value of outcome and the probability of its occurrence.[45] About the same time, a theologian named Antoine Arnauld of France developed the process of statistical inference—making decisions based on a limited set of facts.[46] This is a problem investors know too well today. Thomas Bayes, an English Nonconformist minister laid a more solid foundation for statistical inference in the eighteenth century with the publication of pathbreaking original work on probability, *Essays Towards Solving A Problem In The Doctrine of Chances*. "The primary application of the Bayesian system is in the use of new information to revise probabilities based on old information, or, in the language of statisticians, to compare posterior probability with the priors.... This procedure of revising inference about old information as new information arrives springs from a philosophical viewpoint that makes Bayes's contribution strikingly modern: in a dynamic world, there is no single answer under conditions of uncertainty."[47]

Interest theory and practice is an area where the three issues of time, risk, and risk diversification come into perpetual play. The interest rate built

---

44. Bernstein, *Against the Gods*, 130–31.
45. Ibid., 69–70.
46. Ibid., 70.
47. Ibid., 132–33; see also 129–30.

into a financial product takes into account the tenure (time) of the loan, the risk of repayment, and the premium to cover potential losses. The medieval debate about usury was not just about interest rates, nor only about exploiting the poor by charging excessive rates when they are desperate for resources, but also about the moral question of who owns time. If time belongs to God, are human beings permitted to profit from it by charging interest for the passage of time? The usurer was selling time that rightly belonged to God and to make matters worse the usurer's money worked round the clock, not stopping even on Sabbath days.[48] While the medieval Church has been berated for its doctrine on usury, which militated against development of capital markets, it has not been given credit for developing the theory of interest that underlies modern financial industry. The scholastics in their efforts to deal with issues raised by usury in day-to-day life, especially risk of potential loss to lenders, developed a sophisticated understanding of interest rate theory. They distinguished between actual loss and forgone gains (opportunity cost of lending). In the mid-twentieth century, Joseph Schumpeter accredited them with origin of the modern theory of interest for their understanding of interest as a monetary phenomenon, interest as part of the price of money, and for relating positive interest to business profits.[49]

Another development arose during the debates and the refinements of the notions of interest and usury that have decisively shaped the ethos of modern financial business. In biblical times usury was prohibited among citizens of Israel, among "one's own kind." It was the theological debates of medieval times that shifted the focus from "communal brotherhood" to everybody.[50] This shift is very important as it supports the idea that a bank or investment should trade equally with everybody. According to Max Stackhouse:

> In effect, this shift made every "other" a brother or sister in moral terms, and every brother and sister an "other" in business relationships. A banker ought to exercise fiduciary responsibility in regard to the resources of each customer, and ought not give special rates to those to whom she or he is related. A business should trade with all who will do so peacefully, and should not discriminate

---

48. Taylor, *Confidence Games*, 72–74.

49. Schumpeter, *History of Economic Analysis*, 104–5. See also Ekelund et al, *Sacred Trust*, 128, 177.

50. B. Nelson, "Taking of Interest," 265–71.

racially. These are ideas that had to be established in long and painful battles.[51]

It was John Calvin's work that represented a real turning point in the debate about usury, laying one of the important foundations for the global financial system. He legitimated usury by offering a revision of the inherited exegesis of Deuteronomy and other texts that deal on usury. According to Benjamin Nelson:

> Calvin on Deuteronomy became a Gospel of the modern era. Everyone from the sixteenth to the nineteenth century who advocated a more liberal usury law turned to Calvin for support.... If today we do not appeal to his teachings, it is because we have learned his lessons too well. Religious or even ethical vocabulary is no longer needed to justify the moral and economic postulates which he helped to establish.[52]

The financial products and transactions generated from the interplay of time, risk, and risk management are recorded and interpreted by accounting methods. Records of financial dealings are kept and reported to the internal and external publics in the form of asset/liability, credit and debit. Theologians influenced the early history of accounting, especially double entry bookkeeping. Although he did not invent the idea of double entry bookkeeping, it was Luca Paccioli, a Franciscan monk who popularized the idea.[53] He treated the subject extensively in his 1494 masterwork, *Summa de arithmetic, geometria et proportionalita*. This simple medieval idea of structure of binary opposition, debit and credit that net to zero, has moved from just being a tool for record keeping to being at the very heart of all financial products created and sold in the twentieth and twenty-first centuries. Martin Shubik observes that "financial instruments are always created in pairs that net to zero."[54] At the end of the twentieth century, a prominent financial writer and asset-manager on Wall Street, reviewing this innovation in accounting methods, stated that its economic consequences are comparable to the discovery of the steam engine three hundred years later.[55]

---

51. Stackhouse, "Moral Roots," 36. See also B. Nelson, *Idea of Usury*.

52. B. Nelson, "Taking of Interest," 269.

53. The notion had first appeared in a book published by an Italian firm based in London in 1305.

54. Shubik, *Theory of Money*, 282.

55. Bernstein, *Against the Gods*, 42.

Summary and Concluding Thoughts

This essay has examined the ways in which theological ideas have interacted with other ideas, social structures, and forces to fashion the global financial architecture, products, and operating systems. The aim is to show that the global financial system has arisen within the milieu of Judeo-Christian ethos and thus it cannot be understood by analyzing material forces alone. We need to also pay attention to the religious and ethical values that pervade the social ethos of the global financial system.[56]

The "rationalizing" attitude that governs the modes of production and distribution of investable capital are centered in the ethos of banking and investment houses. The ethos, as Max Weber reminds us, was born and sustained by religious values that he calls the "spirit" of capitalism. Today, important elements of Christian ethos and social teaching have been mixed with modern financial thought to such a degree that they are not recognized as having come from Christian theology. Finance may not use the terms God or providence but it maintains belief in providence: the efficient market hypothesis with its emphasis on automatic harmony and omniscience is providence called by another name. Its idea of market as a place where opposite valuations (bid and offer prices) meet and are resolved into a single valuation for an item may not be far from Nicholas of Cusa's idea of God as the "coincidence of opposites." Nor is it far from Hegel's divine "cunning" of ideas with the notion that the price-value of a commodity uses the vital forces of supply and demand of numerous people in order to realize itself. The theory of the market and its unpredictability are no myth; rather it is a "paradoxical expression for faith in providence," in its capitalist metamorphosis. "The believer in the traditional idea of providence also knew that the ways of providence are dark, contradictory, and obscure; nevertheless, he believed in it and was certain that it would arrive at its goal."[57]

We did not survey all of the complex forces that have shaped the modern financial system, but offered a selection of a few key presupposed themes and the theologically driven "spirit" that has distinctly shaped them.[58] This is not to say that the ethos of the global financial system has

---

56. Stackhouse, *Public Theology*, 87.

57. Tillich, *Protestant Era*, 12.

58. For instance, we did not address the moral and ethical issues concerning the role of finance capital in empire, slave trade and slavery, colonialism and neocolonialism, war and ecology, and wealth and poverty. Nor did we touch on how multilateral development financial institutions are implicated in the morality or immorality of economic

The Moral Roots of the Global Financial Industry

a single set of causes or that there is a one-to-one connection between the Judeo-Christian heritage and the modern financial system in the West. It is not even necessary to accept my choice of themes to recognize that religious ideas and Christianity as a personal faith of many of the players in the industry throughout the history of its development have had a major impact on institutions and products throughout the whole industry. The Judeo-Christian heritage of the West has given the cultures of the West a *credo* that cannot be ignored even when we seemingly are investigating material aspects of the global financial industry. According to Stackhouse, "the *credo* expresses the essential precipitates, the core commitments, of the culture that guide the perception of and the response to 'material forces.' The material forces have, of course, a kind of independence and autonomy when looked at alone, but when it comes to human responses to these forces, *credos* become highly influential."[59]

The overarching conclusion is that the current standard account of the modern financial system that derives from purely material causes has to be revised. We can no longer neglect the fact that the roots of the modern global monetary and financial system are substantially embedded in cultural ethos.

---

development (underdevelopment) in the Majority World. By not addressing them here I am not suggesting they are not important.

59. Stackhouse, *Ethics and the Urban Ethos*, 81.

CHAPTER 9

Theological-Ethical Critique of Accounting

Introduction

WE HAVE SEVERAL TIMES in this book discussed the philosophical underpinnings of accounting. The social practice of accounting has a particular view of the world, which is founded on two key philosophical ideas. First, is the idea that an organization is a unit, a single entity that can be identified in and of itself. The organization is an entity that can be succinctly distinguished from others and a set of accounts can be kept to recognize and record its activities. Second, there is the notion that equality is the fundamental principle in the organization's life: assets must exactly match liabilities (*Assets = Equities; Assets = Liabilities + Owners' Equity*). The whole process of measuring, recording, and reporting the transactions of an entity must always end up with this equality. The social practice of accounting takes the form of ideas and principles that are clearly based on or warranted by this set of central convictions. Any effort to understand the mindset and "social ethics" of accounting as a profession or discipline in itself must recognize the critical significance of its particular view of the world.

This chapter is a reflection on the arithmetic foundation of equality and its ethical and theological contexts. The aim is to open it to ethics and ethical critique. As the pastor learns to use the techniques of accounting and endeavors to think like the accountant for the sake of financial management of the church it is important for her to recognize the mindset and philosophical underpinning of the discipline. This is necessary if she is not to fall prey to the orientation of management that wants to transform *praxis* into *techne*, to build guardrails and protective shields around all human

Theological-Ethical Critique of Accounting

actions so as to shape and mold them for commerce and profit, fashion them into techniques of money-making.

Despite the alluring beauty, simplicity, and neatness of accounting, it should be seen as representing a flight from the frailty, fragility and contingency of human actions, freedom of life in the spirit "into the comfort of the universal, the security of law and order, of rules and structures."[1] The fundamental equation is the epistemological and political *arche* of the order accounting has established over business operations and how it seeks to maintain it. Accounting has no intention either to transform or to transcend the world. All this should not be construed as meaning that accounting is diametrically opposed to the philosophy of ministerial leadership, but only to alert the pastor to keep both accounting and theology in tension.

The Accounting Equation

The accounting equation is the fundamental framework that informs thinking in accounting. The basic reasoning, which flows from the concept of double entry, is that an inevitable principle of duality permeates all transactions in the corporation; there must always be a balance, symmetry between assets and liabilities (plus owners' equity). The transactions of a firm—at least its recording—must always be at equilibrium, or a series of equilibrium moving toward a general equilibrium at the end of the accounting period only to start all over again. Balance debits and credits, and start all over again as long as the entity is a going concern.

Accounting with its unmistakable belief in the universal code of debit and credit, striving for absolute knowledge of equality, is an enactment of a totalizing will. This universalizing will is also a will to truth. The fundamental accounting equation implies a concept of truth. Truth is a correspondence between facts and sayings (written records). This is not only reflected by the "equals to" (=) sign between assets and liability, but also in the idea that what is reported on both sides of the ledger corresponds to reality. With this watertight notion of truth, with every credit matched to a debit, every giving corresponding to a taking, there is no logic of gift or grace that exceeds the circuit of compensation; nor can there be any transaction that can transcend the very measure of exchange or escape return.

---

1. Caputo, *Against Ethics*, 111.

The concept of truth implicit in accounting works with an implied philosophy of language. Uncovering this will require some effort at hermeneutical decoding. The idea behind accounting reports, financial statements is that behind the records ("the said") there are real situations and real events, which exist objectively, fully, and discretely. As accountants qua accountants, when we read reports or records we should be willing to restore the numbers to a source, to real object, real event having a definite form. The reports speak about real entities; they are real presentations of persons, transactions, situations, or matter called the thing-in-itself. They are not mere linguistic artifacts.

There are problems with this assumption of real presence in the reports. The assumption ignores the fact that the very existence of the reports is based on absence; the reports enact a representation and indeed come into existence to stand-in for what is essentially absent before the readers. For accountants, reports become "no more than glass panes behind which events occur." But we must counter this problematic reading, this *passive reading*, this *epi-reading* of reports with some wisdom from Jacques Derrida on textuality. He writes that it is necessary to "take into account the process of vitrification and not discount the 'production' of the glass. The production does not consist . . . simply in unveiling, revealing, presenting; nor in concealing or causing to disappear all at once . . . The glass must be read as a text."[2] This is precisely what the idealistic philosophy of accounting does not want us to do. We are simply required to find the significance of the entity "behind the screen" of the accounting language, the said. In fact for the accountant's way of thinking, language does not exist: real situations and real events "shine through like light through a perfect window." On the contrary, we might assume that "language operates as a plane of glass that it is impossible to see through and might, in fact, be a screen with nothing behind it."[3] The work of a good financial analyst is to decode the said, to resist the pressure of the said, but not with the intention of reaching a space beyond language, only to deconstruct the reports and enter into a dialogue with them.

---

2. Derrida, *Dissemination*, 233, quoted in Eaglestone, *Ethical Criticism*, 46.

3. Eaglestone, *Ethical Criticism*, 94.

Theological-Ethical Implications of the Accounting Equation

Each of these features of accounting we have discussed carries ethical and theological corollaries. As is often the case, novelists got to this point before academic philosophers and theologians. Charles Dickens in his novel, *Little Dorrit* (1857), partly about the institutions of debtors' prisons in nineteenth-century Britain, appears to have understood this connection very well. The central protagonist, Arthur Clennam on returning to London after many years of living abroad, wondered if his family owed someone something. When he got into the claustrophobic liar in which his stepmother had imprisoned herself, he asks "is it possible, mother, that he [father] had unhappily wronged any one, and made no reparation?"[4] This question is based on his familiarity with logic of gain and pain, every debit must be settled for the moral economy to be in harmony. In this system every guilt must be expatiated.

Mrs. Clennam, Arthur's stepmother, conceptualized guilt and punishment as a system of economic exchange. In the world of this Dickens' novel, the ground norm of accounting—that is, all debits and credits must ultimately balance—is the principle that informs the handling of personal and societal ethics and guilt. The authorial voice of Dickens put this clearly to the reader in its assessment of Mrs. Clennam who waffled when Arthur asked for a line-by-line description of her crimes: "Thus she was always balancing her bargains with the Majesty of heavens, posting up the entries to her credit, strictly keeping her set-off, and claiming her due. She was only remarkable in this, for the force and emphasis with which she did it. Thousands upon thousands do it, according to their varying manner, every day."[5] According to literary scholar Daniel Born:

> In Mrs. Clennam, Dickens created a being who makes no distinction whatsoever between her moral and financial entries, and her self-imprisonment is, in her view, the self-inflicted pain meant to balance out the pain she knows she has dealt to others: first, the suppression of the will entitling Little Dorrit to a legacy, and the second, the casting out of the illegitimate son Arthur. The second action she perceives as justifiable in light of the pain she has suffered for being forced to marry his father. Pain suffered, as Nietzsche observes, demands equal infliction of pain on someone else, and the target for that infliction of pain finally does not

---

4. Dickens, *Little Dorritt*, 35.
5. Ibid., 37.

matter—just so long as the requisite damage is done to balance the books overall.[6]

Let us further deepen our investigations of theological and ethical implications of the ground norm and other salient features of accounting by focusing on the category of faith. In accounting the basis of faith is mental assent to some propositions about accounting, GAAP (generally accepted accounting principles) and the inevitable concomitant practices that flow from them. This is how faith in a corporation's financial statement is gained and maintained. This kind of faith is all about assurance, convincing the public as much as it is possible that there is a real *sub-stance* behind the numbers. But Jean-Luc Nancy informs us that Christian faith is neither about economy of assurances or substitutes for assurance, nor about adherence to some contents of belief without proof or leap beyond proof. "It is an act by a person of faith, an act that, as such, is the attestation by an intimate consciousness to the fact that it exposes itself and allows itself to be exposed to the absence of attestation, of *parousia*."[7] Though accounting faith requires attestation—usually provided by auditors—it does not dispense forgiveness to its faithful.

The basic accounting equation is very unforgiving, uncompromising. One does not need to see hapless clerks laboring in the dead of the night over trial balance that will not balance because of a few pennies to understand my point. One also does not need to go far afield to recognize that the arithmetic equation is strictly for one entity at a time, separate and distinguishable for which a set of accounts can be kept. The boundaries of this entity are rigidly delimited, set off from all others. Separateness, discreteness is what defines "personhood" and not interconnectedness and mutuality.

One only needs to recognize the discipline, diligence, and dedication with which zero as the solution to assets minus liabilities is pursued and obtained in the whole network of ledgers. Let us remember that according to the accounting equation, asset = equity (liability), and this translates to asset − equity = 0. The fundamental thought here is that relationship is a zero-sum game. How could this not be? If all resource contribution and outlays must be exactly matched and balanced, then there is no excess, no non-zerosumness in economic (social) interactions and encounters

---

6. Born, *Birth of Liberal Guilt*, 40–41.
7. Nancy, *Dis-Enclosure*, 153; italics in the original.

between entities. Yet we know that there are synergies and excesses in relations between entities (persons) and in economic encounters.

The accounting equation is based on the principle of reciprocity. This obviates any openness to the possibility of the unexpected or exuberance. Some may regard this kind of austerity as negating or thwarting life. Relationships that work only on the principle of reciprocity are bound to the magic of equivalent results and strict repayments. Strict adherence to reciprocity in any relationship drives it to death, making it "an automatic reflex with much more in common with magic than classical Christian faith."[8]

The principle of reciprocity is also what undergirds the prosperity gospel. The reasoning is that believers give to God and God is obligated to bless them in return. "In other words, the message of salvation by grace alone, implying the impossibility of reciprocity with God, is often forgotten when the offering plate is being passed."[9] The principle of reciprocity has permeated much of American life. Often we do not realize that even as Christians or believers the whole of our life operates on this principle. That is to say, our way of being is that of a bookkeeper or what Yale University theologian Miroslav Volf, following Natalie Davies, calls life in the "sales mode." Our life—relationship, thinking, and doing—appears stuck in the market mode, searching for equivalent exchange, fair prices for our products, services, and efforts. When we invite someone for dinner into our homes we expect them to reciprocate at some point. And if he fails we remind him that it is bad manners not to reciprocate. "The sales mode refers to the market of buying and selling. Here we give something in order to *get* a rough equivalent in exchange."[10] Because we are embedded in this mode of existence in the United States, clergy and other Christians do not live their lives in the "gift mode." The gift mode "refers to relations between donors and recipients. Here we *give* favors that we don't owe and the recipients don't deserve. If recipients returns favors, they do so unforced, after a time lag, and in a different form."[11]

Following Davies, Volf describes three modes in which human beings relate to one another. We have already discussed two of them: sales and gift. The third is the "coercive mode." "The coercive mode refers to various forms of theft. In this mode, we *take* what is not ours and what is not being

---

8. J. Jamieson and P. Jamieson, *Ministry and Money*, 162.
9. Ibid.
10. Volf, *Free of Charge*, 57; italics in the original.
11. Ibid.

offered to us. Armed with insider information, we sell our stocks before it tumbles down, and the hapless buyers take the loss. Or to use a more innocent example, at work we slip a pen into our pocket and take it home."[12] The accounting equation does not support the coercive mode; it is about legitimate acquisitions. It is an equation born of the exchange mode. But Christian ethics goes beyond the exchange mode, demanding believers to live in the gift mode, to give generously. The gift mode preserves and promotes community. "A gift is a social relations, not an entity or act in itself. It is an event *between* people. . . . Gifts don't just happen between people; they also serve 'to create, nourish, or re-create social bonds.'"[13] As explained by Volf we find the three basic categories in scripture:

> Ephesians 4 shows us how to order our lives, how to live as new selves rather than as old. In the process of contrasting the old life and the new, the text speaks briefly of all three modes mentioned—taking, acquiring or getting, and giving. In particular, verse 28 reads: "Thieves must give up stealing; rather let them labor and work honestly with other own hands, so as to have something to share with the needy."[14]

I need to quickly add that neither Volf nor this writer is against getting. The difference between what we are advocating and what the accounting equation proposes or endorses is that while we believe that getting and giving are not mutually exclusive alternatives, accountancy considers them exclusive.[15] People must work to get money, capability, or some resource to give so they can become channels of God's gifts. The accounting entity by definition is always a getter and never allowing itself to become a giver. The entity in its expression as a business corporation is wired to maximize profits through all legitimate means. In the rare occasion that it gives out of character it is for the sake of getting.

The accounting equation is philosophically opposed to the gift mode of life—or at least is not open to it. For instance, the accounting worldview cannot make sense of Abraham's willingness to murder his son Isaac in obedience to God, to heed the "absolute request of the other." Such a commitment, absolute responsibility to God, does not make sense as it has no promise of reciprocal payment. Abraham's response to the request,

12. Ibid., 56; italics in the original.
13. Ibid., 84; italics in the original.
14. Ibid., 57.
15. Ibid., 58.

Theological-Ethical Critique of Accounting

as Jacques Derrida puts it as he interprets Kierkegaard's reflection on the request, stands in a relationship of "absolute singularity." The accounting equation as a particular interpretation of responsibility is not aporetic; it is relative and foundational. There is an irreducible ground of repayments, quid pro quo, from which all responsibility emerges. The accounting notion of responsibility, in my reading, is ultimately based on a "physics" of presence. It is based on the presence of being, a thing, physical and immanent, which is willing to truck, barter, and exchange as the ultimate source of human responsibility. The accounting notion of responsibility recognizes an attachment to objects that act as ballast, capable of delivering the actor from the full weight of her burden. Responsibility is not the absence of anchors, not acceptance of life in freedom. It is always a balancing act whether it is on a high wire or on *terra firma*.

The moral responsibility that the accounting equation recognizes is one that does not seek anything above itself. Responsibility is grounded in the encounter of the pair, both sides of the equation. Both sides represent real objects, events or situation, the thing-in-itself. Responsibility is about obligations ongoing earthly entities owe to one another. This view of responsibility rejects generosity and disdain acting that is not a matter of a knowable plan. This puts the accounting view at odds with some of the dominant views of ethics in church and academic circles. An ethics of generosity is transgressive of the protection that this notion of responsibility affords. According to John D. Caputo, "the affirmation of 'responsibility,' 'ethics,' 'decision' . . . will never be a matter of knowledge . . . , of a determinable program, a knowable plan, of planning ahead, but a generosity, a gift that gives without return—whenever it is called for, whenever the occasion calls for it."[16] Theologians and philosophers believe that generosity, not strict balancing of scales, is the key to building and maintaining social relationships in a beloved community and in promoting justice, which is about the quality of communal relationships.

The particular mindset that thrives on balancing debits and credits, looking for ways to offset costs with revenues, and on balancing the books desiccates all social ties and relationships. The virtue and health of human relationships are reduced to arithmetic problems of balancing books, matching revenues to expenses. Take the case of Michael Rice, a Walmart employee who had a heart attack at his workplace while helping a customer, and died a week later. Unbeknownst to him and his surviving wife Walmart

---

16. Caputo, *Deconstruction in a Nutshell*, 123.

had taken a life insurance policy on him and named itself as the beneficiary. When he died the company collected $300,000. When his wife, Vicki Rice questioned Walmart, the explanation was that it makes a considerable investment to train its workers and the company only comes out ahead if they continued to live. But if employees die untimely, the company needs to cover its costs of training. The insurance payouts then enable the company to cover its losses and pay for the replacement of deceased employees. According to a Walmart spokesman, "He [Michael Rice] has been given quite a bit of training and gained experience that cannot be duplicated without costs."[17] The statement of Walmart should not just be seen as poor public relations, but for what it is, a strategy of corporate finance riding on the formidable urge to balance all books.

The accounting equation points us to the fundamental nature of accounting as a system of obligations. (Obligations—from *ligare, ob-ligare, re-ligare*—are binding; you cannot get past them.) The bookkeeping method is graceless, perpetuating a relationship that maps debtors and creditors, quantifying who owes what to whom. This view of relationship between entities or transactions—balancing debts and credits, costs and rewards—enfolds a view of ethics or life that rejects ethical relationship between unequals. In its lights the right relationship is irreducibly symmetrical, reciprocal. Justice is the balancing of scales.

All this reminds us of Friedrich Nietzsche's argument in *The Genealogy of Morals* (1887). The word, *Schulde* (guilt), according to him is related to *Schulden*, the material concept of debt. Bookkeeping is the accounting equivalent of ethical scorekeeping. The practice of bookkeeping in morality insists that the infliction of pain on an offender is the moral compensation for any fracture of relationship or moral code. Primitive ethics, in Nietzsche's thought, is a form of double entry bookkeeping. In the philosophy of accounting, which as we have seen strives for absolute equality, forever matching pain to reward, we can easily sense the connection between moral conscience and monetary exchange. Nietzsche makes this amply clear in this passage:

> For an unconscionably long time culprits were not punished because they were felt to be responsible for their actions; not, that is, on the assumption that only the guilt were to be punished; rather, they were punished the way parents still punish their children, out of rage at some damage suffered, which the doer must pay for.

17. Sandels, *What Money Can't Buy*, 132.

> Yet this rage was both moderated and modified by the notion that for every damage that could somehow be found an equivalent, by which that damage might be compensated—if necessary in the pain of the doer. To the question how that ancient, deep-rooted, still firmly established notion of an equivalency between damage and pain arise, the answer is, briefly: it arose in the contractual relations between debtor and creditor, which is as old as the notion of "legal subjects" itself and which in its turn points back to the basic practices of purchase, sale, barter, and trade.[18]

The equality, the discipline demanded by accounting, is often harsh. Because all thoughts revolve around equilibrium, creative imagination (not necessarily shenanigans) threatens to bring its whole vision of economic life down with it. The dominance of a thinking anchored to equality of input and output, going-in and going-out—indeed a closed system—gives no place to a radical alternative to the present mindset, only making ample room for the mere ratification of existing harmony. Equality as the *ultimate concern* in the social practice of accounting has a contestatory relationship with grace, and considers as odd every principle, belief, or practice that accents grace. Indeed, given the rigorous and uncompromising standard of this jealous ultimate concern any deviation is tantamount to "moral and spiritual degradation." You can be rest assured such infractions will be transferred to the debits and credits of the eternal accountant's ledger.

The accent of the accounting equation on equality, reciprocity, obligation, and careful balancing of scales points to the fundamental ethics of accounting as ethics of *calculability*, the calculability of obligations. The corporate actor, qua business, does not transcend its obligations to the other. The cost, loss of resources, is calculated ahead of time and it is redeemable. Its chosen form of ethics is not a disruptive one. It is about carefully tracing out the cycle of debt and there is nothing absolutely aleatory about it as Emmanuel Levinas or Derrida would like us to consider. As Derrida argues in his book, *The Gift of Death* the ethical demand, the responsibility toward the other, the *tout autre*, compels us to renounce "every human law," to behave ir-responsibly in the face of such law:

> In a word, ethics must be sacrificed in the name of duty. It is a duty not to respect, out of duty, ethical duty. One must behave not only in an ethical or responsible manner, but in a nonethical, nonresponsible manner, and one must do that *in the name* of duty, of an

---

18. Nietzsche, *"Genealogy of Morals,"* 195.

> infinite duty, *in the name of* absolute duty. And this name, which must always be singular, is here none other than the name of God as completely other [God as a place-holder for the absolutely other], the nameless name of God, the unpronounceable name of God as other to which I am bound by an absolute, unconditional obligation, by an incomparable, nonnegotiable duty.[19]

Philosophical Thought and the Accounting Equation

Upon careful reflection, the fundamental accounting equation brings to mind the ancient Greek concept of justice, *dikê*. Injustice is an imbalance and justice is what rights the balance. Justice is understood as an exceptionless, inflexible retribution. So in the archaic conception of justice, even the changes in the seasons were interpreted as cosmic balancing acts of compensation for encroachment. Winter invades the domain of the warm and dry with its cold and wet, grasping more than its share, and it is offset by summer, which squeezes out cold and wet. So the philosopher Anaximander writing about the seasons in sixth-century BC puts it: "They pay penalty and retribution (*dikên kai tisin*) to one another in accordance with the assessment of time."[20]

The accounting equation, as we have seen pursues strict proportional balancing; any wrong or right (debit or credit) must be righted in one symmetrical process of getting the right amount and getting the amount right. This is exactly the world of *dikê*, the primitive sense of justice and morality. As Martha Nussbaum puts it:

> The world of strict *dike* is a harsh and symmetrical world in which order and design are preserved with exceptionless clarity. After summer comes fall, after fall comes winter, after day comes the night.... It is a world in which gods are home, and in which mortals often fare badly. As a fragment of Sophocles puts it, "The god before whom you come ... knows neither equity nor grace (*oute toupieikes oute tên charin*), but only cares for strict and simple justice (*tên haplôs dikên*)." The world of *epieikeia* or equity, by contrast, is a world of imperfect human efforts and complex obstacles to doing well.[21]

---

19. Derrida, *Gift of Death*, 67.
20. Anaximander DK fragment B, quoted Nussbaum, *Sex and Social Justice*, 157.
21. Nussbaum, *Sex and Social Justice*, 159; italics in the original.

From ancient Greek thought and Nussbaum let us shift our focus to modern Hegelian thought and Slavoj Žižek to further reveal the hidden ethico-theological dimensions of the fundamental accounting equation. Once again, let us start from the basic thought. The accounting equation is Asset = Liability = Asset − Liability equals to zero (= 0). The question now is: Is asset *not-liability* or *non-liability*? Put differently, is liability not-asset or non-asset?[22]

Liability as not-asset is a negation of the predicate. As a negation of a predicate, it is seen as a purely negative situation, having no positive force. If liability is not-asset it means liability has no reality apart from asset, apart from the way it is affected by asset. If liability is not-asset it then means that Asset − Liability = 0, as it is usual to assert. But it says something more. The zero here means either asset or liability is totally at rest, totally passive when it comes to a balance with the other. Zero in this case is a gesture of immobilization.

Liability as non-asset is not a negation of the predicate. So it is not "this is not an asset," but this is a non-asset. Zero in this case opens up a space for movement and transformation. How we read the equation in terms of the relation between asset and liability is crucial in interpreting the constituting/constitutive dynamics of accounting thought. It is also important for understanding how accounting thought interprets reality. For us to develop a philosophy of accounting we cannot merely appeal to immediate reality or pragmatic operations of balancing the books. Only a rigorous conceptual thinking of this matter can adequately situate and explicate the philosophy of accounting.

On the whole the fundamental accounting equation makes a very interesting philosophical, unexpected dialectical point. Asset (liability) can only be properly understood through its difference to its opposite. If asset is not graspable its opposite, not-asset (liability) is also not knowable, and vice versa. The external opposition between asset and liability by virtue of their positing by the equals-to sign shows that there is always already an internal gap within each of them. One is always the form of appearance of the other. The possession rights of assets are the forms of appearance of the obligations of liabilities. The identity of asset (liability) is split from within. The tension between being one or the other (opposite) is inherent to the particular identity of each of them.

---

22. The philosophical analyses of this section of the chapter was inspired by Žižek, *Less than Nothing*.

Debit and credit within the records of asset (liability) merely materialize this inherent split. In accounting there is nothing like knowing a transaction *in-itself*, it is always "for us," as it appears in relation to otherness, to its opposite entry. The external difference between asset and liability is always internal to each of them. The external limitation of asset to liability is always reflected in the field of debit and credit within each of them, as its inherent impossibility of fully becoming the One, of fully generating the totality of entries out of itself without the traces of the other within it. To know then is to accept this limitation, and the impossibility of stepping outside of it. Far from this limitation separating the accountant from the reality of the given transaction, it bears witness to certain recognition of reality. The accountant does not recognize excess reality over any transaction insofar as knowing amounts to a radical closure (balance, equality).

The basic insight here is that the external opposition between asset and liability is grounded in asset's (liability's) immanent self-opposition. While the fundamental equation rests on agreement, harmony of thought (being) with itself, the unit of transaction (reality) around which this thought circulates is always already split. We can never know the transaction in itself (i.e., there is epistemological indeterminacy), we are condemned to know it as defined by the radical finitude of the correlation between debit and credit which separates us from the "core" of transaction, if there is such a thing.

The pure beauty of accounting thought is not to bypass this split identity of object to reach the thing-in-itself, but to assert the limitation and draw out all its consequences for organizing financial information, decision-making, and corporate management. The difference between the claim of absolute knowability of the fundamental equation and the finite knowledge of debit and credit is transposed back into the basic principle of debit and credit, as the split between the "gentrified," self-identical asset (liability) and the impossibility of having harmonious identity of transaction that is sutured by debit and credit entries.

The acceptance of the limitation (epistemological indeterminacy) means that the inability to know is a fundamental feature or property of reality, which is also indeterminate. So the epistemology of accounting is also ontology. What precludes our access, despite the transparency and harmony of the fundamental equation, to the reality of transaction is *reality itself*.

Money and the Accounting Equation

The fundamental relationship of equality between asset and equity defines one as means and the other as the end. Equities/liabilities provided by owners and lenders are the means for securing assets. On the other hand, the assets are the representation of the equities/liabilities, the means of knowing their deployment.

Asset and equity are always interlocked in multiple byways and every way. One always means the other. Equity means asset and asset means equity. They are engaged with one another as sign and meaning, signifier and signified. Depending on your perspective, asset is a sign of equity and also the signified. You can say the same thing about equity.

Thus, the accountant's viewpoint presents a semantic reading of the interrelationships between the resource-contributors of the corporation, which inevitably adopts correspondence as the default mode of analysis, the matching of equivalents. This kind of matching and correspondence requires a *general equivalent of value*, a notion or norm of value more abstract than the objects compared. The simple one-to-one correspondence in accountancy depends on money as the abstract notion of value, a general equivalent for anything and everything. One can now say—without any surprise—that ultimately money is the supreme value ordering and directing the fundamental principle of equality, which is the ultimate concern of accounting as a social practice. The god of accounting bows before the god of money!

So no theology (philosophy) or theological-ethical critique of accounting can be adequately forged without an overarching theology/philosophy of money. Money (as the facilitator of exchange which may appear as hard cash or paper in modern economy or remain invisible in barter economy) stands behind the practice of accounting as its guarantee, transcendent value.

This close connection between money and accounting, more precisely the accounting equation, should not blind us to seeing contradictions between the two. While the recording of money as medium of exchange, as instrument for economic transactions, is about balance, presenting static snapshots, money itself is about the inherent dynamism of 0 *and* 1, which it encapsulates. Accounting is about dead transactions or at best a living dead. It must do its work after the flight of the Minerva (Main Street) owl, looking down on dead transactions. It is a coroner's kind of job. Money is the facilitator thick with life, pulsating social practices of business. Records are formal, dead, barren. Money quickens and record, the dead letter, gathers its end-of-life stories.

Financial instruments exist and die in the world of paired zeros and ones. Financial products and transactions are created, recorded, interpreted, and retired by accounting methods, a system of binary opposition, debit and credit that net to zero. Records of financial dealings are kept and reported to internal and external publics in the form of asset and liability or credit and debit.

Money is both 0 and 1, outside and inside, being (presence) and non-being (absence, void, emptiness). To have a presence is to be "counted-as-one," to be counted as part of a structured set (*multiple* conceived as a set), to belong to a *situation*,[23] to be presented as a result of the process of one-ification, and to have time and space.[24] It is to be finite. To have zero is not to have a presence but marked by the boundary of presence. The unpresented, the unpresentable, (the not-yet) cannot be counted as part of a *situation*, but exists as the *void*-part, "the part of no-part" of every situation and haunts it. This void is not in a far-off place. It figures from within every situation purely and simply as *margin*.[25] The zero (the nothing, the *void*, the null set in Alain Badiou's thought) is the fount of possibilities. The one is conditioned, limited, and originated from the multiplicity that is zero; that zero that is infinite.

The count is a result of a structuring process of a multiplicity. In the multiplicity from which the one is structuredly counted there is a remainder "over and beyond the horizon that circumscribes the situation"; and this is "a necessary implication of the (counting or structuring) operation that makes the situation what it is."[26] There is always an immeasurable

---

23. See Badiou, *Being and Event*. "First, whatever is presented must be presented as one, that is, it must be structured in such a way that it can be counted as one: Badiou defines a situation, in the most general sense, as the result of any such structuring or counting operation. To exist is to belong to a situation, and within any situation there is normally no chance of encountering anything unstructured, that is, anything that cannot be counted as a one. Second, we know nonetheless that this operation is a result, and that whatever was thus structured or counted as one is not itself one, but multiple." Hallward, *Badiou*, 64.

24. "The present implies space. Time creates the present through its union with space. In this union time comes to a standstill because there is something on which to stand. Like time, space unites being with nonbeing. . . . To be means to have space." Tillich, *Systematic Theology*, 1:194.

25. This for Badiou is the "immanent excess of parts over elements."

26. Hallward, *Badiou*, 64–65.

excess of parts over elements in all human situations. "But because it is unrepresentable, this multiplicity must figure from within the situation purely and simply as nothing."[27] The irreducible excess of parts over elements in any set counted as one means that the finite can extend itself in potentially infinite ways. But that which can be part of all sets is the *void*, the null set in set theoretic terms.

The *void* is the absent "no-thing" upon which the innovative financial agent acts (intervenes) to present something, an invention of something new, and new criterion for action. What is presented is not always good or can be immediately recognized as part of the extant situation. According to Badiou the *void* is characterized by a condition of indifference as it does not "belong" to any situation and is always threatening to subvert it. Financial innovators produce the new by encountering the aspect of an extant figuration that has no interest in preserving the status quo as such. The innovator is the one who makes "no-thing" appear in the surface of existing forms of financial sociality and then proclaims the new.

All this insight has implication for how we understand the ontology of money and financial innovation. Financial product is a coupling of what is known in the established symbolic order and what is missing, an object of desire, inspiration, or *event* to use Badiou language. The zero is the dynamic part of the 0 + 1 static and dynamic dimension of all monetary existence. The zero in money is always present, but it is unrepresentable, always not presented. It is there in every situation of financial product but its elements cannot be known within the situation. The existing situation obscures it, but then from time to time some elements emerge as the "impossible" of the situation to re-configure the situation—create a new situation. It is thus the groundless ground of financial innovation and creativity. The zero is "the unknowable point, action in the product or system that converts the impossible into the possible."[28]

The Prophetic Voice and the Accounting Equation

The paired zero and one can be interpreted as natality and potentiality (the miracle of the new and the not-yet) versus mortality and actualization. The principle of double entry, accounting is about actualization, but the

---

27. Ibid., 66.
28. Ibid., 14.

principle of money is about potentiality. In this limited sense, zero and one is about money and accounting, money and its record.

We have repeatedly argued at various portions of the book leading up to this moment and we will further argue that money is a form of social relation. Money is about social relationality, living and pulsating encounters of human beings in various forms of sociality. The dynamism of money is about the dynamism of human interactions. Accounting is about the record of the sediments and deposits of such interactions and encounters. But often the structures and ethics that guide the production and distribution of money in the whole economy are not life-giving enough to the collective economic existence of all classes in the society. The monetary structures and general market system begin to create crushing inequalities and other forms of injustice that limits the participation of the poor in the economy.

Often these ills are worsened by monetary policy that does not do its work. Monetary policy is the mobilization of an economy's monetary and financial resources for the preservation, promotion, and ordering of its work. Productive and reproductive work—organization and distribution of rewards thereof—maintains the structure of mutuality of life through which a people shape their lives and cope with their day-to-day problems. But monetary policy can and do often eat away at the core forms of relationality that hold the social fabric of this country.

In order to correct or address these social problems the nation needs several prophetic voices. The prophets need to act in ways that can move the monetary system to realize its potentiality, and hence more actualization toward flourishing community life. Prophets as critical voices exist in the gap between potentiality and actualization and their actions in mobilizing their communities will not only influence the past by igniting past actualities in the present, but also structure the future. This task is not about searching for a perfect or readymade solution to current predicaments, but looking at the sparks of possibilities in the structures and ethics of the monetary system and blowing upon them. In the next chapter, we will attempt to forge a relational theology of money that might help the various prophetic voices in this task—or at least open up a new theological conversation about money in our community's economic life.

Concluding Remarks: Translating the Message

It is germane to repeat what I said at the beginning of this chapter. The unflattering ethical analyses of the accounting equation should not be construed as meaning that accounting is diametrically opposed to the philosophy of ministerial leadership. There is no safe space where ministers can inhabit and not be affected by the power of accounting, its ground norm. The power cannot be identified with a particular sphere of the society, as might be suggested by some; nor can that power be identified with one profession or way of being, as in standard liberal theological thinking. It pervades the whole of the capitalist system, the totality of modern society; the economy of exchange touches even the church and its theology.

The portrayal of double entry bookkeeping and moral bookkeeping in this chapter tells us something about how certain ground norms penetrate our common consciousness. Let us put aside any debate about whether the philosophy of double entry bookkeeping as invented in the medieval period is merely an expression of certain ideas and practices in religion and culture or it is the influencer of moral thinking that comes in its wake. One thing is clear, the ground norm is not separate from the ethos of the larger culture and it is encoded in the languages of the larger world.

The exposition of the ethical implications of the ground norm, as discussed below, should not be construed to mean that it has a consolidated and homogenous domination over business thinking or that of society. We should keep in mind that profession or occupation is not what makes the difference between those who exclusively base their thinking on the ground norm and those who do not submit to it. The fundamental principle of accounting, if we do not take too distant a view of modern capitalist-market economy, must be analyzed as the power of an idea or orientation which circulates, or rather as something which only functions in concatenation with rationalization of economic activities. So the domination or impact of the fundamental principle is never localized in the accounting, never limited to a discipline or profession. The principle is employed and exercised through all modern economic networks. Not only do individuals (business executives or not) circulate through its threads; they are always in the position of being subjected to and subjecting others to its power. "They are not only its inert or consenting target; they are always also the elements of its articulation. In other words, individuals are the vehicles of [the] power [of the ground norm], not points of application."[29]

So the key to relating with the fundamental equation is not rejecting it outright; for ministry leaders need to learn discipline of efficiency and competence in strategy. One can come to terms with the fundamental equation and yet transcend it. As we learned from theologian Volf, we all need to be getters so as to have the resources to become givers. Thusly, ministerial leaders need to leverage and stretch their resources and relationships to capture or create new opportunities for the flourishing of their people and ministries. This is the way to transcend the rigors of the equation without escaping it—or worse, rejecting it as ungodly.

The transition from getting to giving also requires a bridge. It requires an awareness of social relations as the bedrock upon which getting and giving are both anchored. Gift is a social relations as we learned earlier. Getting is an exchange relation; nay, it is also a social relation. Not only is economic (fair) exchange always embedded in social relations and social structures, it is also a representation of the social relations that exist between people in a given community. A church, a company of worshipers, unlike a business organization has to take very seriously the tendering of the whole garden of social relations in its community. Paying attention to the whole fabric of society demands an awareness or special insight on the one thread that runs through much of the fabric, if not all of it. This all-connecting thread in modern societies is money. We have already given hints that money— the most general equivalent value in all three modes of human interactions: coercive, sales, and gift—is itself a social relation. In a moment we will turn to money and start crafting a theology of money as a social relation.

Since we have argued against a careless rejection of the accounting equation, a question confronts us: How may the minister adopt the *truth* of the accounting equation? Those who believe this truth also believe that the business-cultural specific experience that comes with its faithful application is normative of some "divine" truth in leadership (managerial) competence. It is truth about which they share the missionary zeal to spread its message. Indeed in practice, submitting to the uncompromising rigors of the accounting equation is not only about "upholding the truth but also relationship and communication."[30]

---

29. Foucault, *Power/Knowledge*, 98. In this paragraph I have closely followed Foucault's description to describe the influence of the accounting ground norm.

30. Sanneh, *Translating the Message*, 33.

How may ministerial leadership benefit from the equation? There are two ways, if we may paraphrase ideas developed in the different context of Christian mission by Lamin Sanneh, a Yale University historian. One is to make the business culture the carrier and arbiter of the truth or message of the fundamental equation. I will call this method adoption by *diffusion*. By it the message of the equation expands into the church by means of its founding business-cultural warrants and is implanted in the church as a matter of cultural adoption.[31]

The other is to allow the message to penetrate our understanding of ministerial leadership "without the requirement of deference to the originating culture."[32] This other way regards the church culture as a valid and necessary way of being and a locus of proclamation of a different truth, if not a higher truth. This is adoption by *translation*, and it carries with it the requirement for serious reflection, which is necessary in the process of reception and adaptation.[33] This chapter, indeed the whole book, is an effort toward this necessary but neglected theological inquiry.

---

31. I have adapted Sanneh's words to suit my purpose here. See his *Translating the Message*, 33.

32. Ibid.

33. Ibid., 34.

Chapter 10

A Relational Theology of Money

Introduction

THE DOLLAR IS ESSENTIALLY backed by nothing, no-thing. It is backed by nothing other than itself. The government does not guarantee to give you gold, metal, or any commodity in exchange for the paper. There is no underlying asset and it is not convertible to any asset. You accept papers as payment for your wages and goods because you believe that others will do the same thing. Money has become a pure relationality—all that matters now is general acceptance. What the Federal Reserve Bank promises anyone who holds the dollar are these words: "THIS NOTE IS LEGAL TENDER FOR ALL DEBTS, PUBLIC AND PRIVATE," written on the face of every note. The dollar strives on trust and faith, on social relations, on the generalized system of credit and debit. Social relation is the "something" of which the "nothing" of money made. Social relation is the "stuff of nothing."

This money that the government and Fed enjoin or even compel you to accept in payment for debts, goods, and services, is itself founded on debt, precisely credit-debit relations. The country operates debt money, such that every dollar note out there has a price on its head, so to speak. The Federal Reserve Bank, the central bank of the nation, creates money, "high-power money" by buying government securities from the commercial banks. If the Federal Reserve Board wanted to pump $20 billion into the United States economy, it had to buy that amount of government securities from the banks (creating new bank reserves for them) and pay appropriate interest to the commercial banks or their investors. The Fed cannot just create

A Relational Theology of Money

money as the Treasury Department does with its issuance of metal coins, which is debt-and-interest free.

The monetary transactions, the credit-debit relations are always embedded in social relations between men and women. And credit-debit is also a form of social relations and it is very easy to mistake them for relations between things. Money is not always seen as a relation. Economic sociologists generally claim that social relations significantly influence money. They have identified the social character of money (interpersonal transactions) as one of the key properties of money. Their main point is that money is embedded in social relations. Here, I posit that money *is* a social relation. The point I want to make here is that money is not only embedded in social relations, it is created out of social relations.

Let me provide a quick overview of the arguments that are presented in detail in chapters 2, 3, and 4 of my book, *God and Money: Theology of Money in a Globalizing World*. A monetary medium (metal, electronic transfers, or computer bytes), no matter however it is dematerialized, exists in relation to the social institutions that confer moneyness on it. The identification (the setting apart) of a particular object, physical particle is itself relational. An object (e.g., gold, silver, or tobacco) is brought into certain relationship to serve society as money. Its very existence as money depends on this intentionality of the users, conscious social agents. Every existent monetary medium bears such connection or connections. A physical particle or medium can perform the function of money by virtue of its physical features. But the function is imposed by human beings "only in virtue of a certain form of collective acceptance of the objects as having a certain sort of status. With that status, comes a function, that can only be performed in virtue of the collective acceptance by the community that the object has that status, and that status carries the function with it."[1] During and after an object is constituted by a particular (detachable and depersonalized) configuration of social relations to become or be counted as monetary medium it still exists within the general, overarching social relations of the community. This is to say that the object is always embedded (situated) in complex social relationships, within the network of personal relations and transactions that make up the society. As Carl Wennerlind puts it: "money does not exist in a vacuum but is part of an elaborate web of dynamic social structural conditions within which people act and interact. As such, money is a social relation in the sense that it mediates the interaction between

---

1. Searle, "Social Ontology and Political Power."

people [and it is socially contingent]."[2] The social relations or the social structures that select an object exist even if they are not or yet recognized by all the users of the monetary medium. This is the way to understand what I mean by money being constituted by social relations and being embedded in social relations.

Money as a Social Relation

Let us now provide a socio-historical analysis of money to buttress the above assertion or characterization of money. This will begin by examining the relations between debt and money (capitalist credit-money). Unlike the dominant tradition of neoclassical economic analysis of money, which places the market at the center of money's origin, other traditions like the debt perspective on money put states and banks at the center stage. As Geoffrey Ingham states, "capitalist credit-money was produced by a qualitative transformation in the *social relations of the mode of monetary production*. . . . [It] is nothing more than a network of claims backed by banks' and states' promises to pay that are fabricated into a hierarchy of credibility by foreign exchange markets and global credit rating agencies."[3] How did all this happen?

In medieval Italian city-states like Genoa, Florence, and Venice, state and bank debts became accepted as general means of payment. The debts were guaranteed by the states' ability to impose and collect taxes. These credits, "promises to pay" were detached from commodities and were not a symbolic reflection of any underlying commodity.

These means of payment retained their value not because people expected their convertibility into any metal or commodity. These were just "promises to pay" serving as means of payment, medium of exchange, and depending only on the constitutional legitimacy of the state and institutionalized banking practice. Note that the strength of state theory of money is not that money receives its value from legal tender laws, but from the legal requirement of its citizens to pay taxes; that is, on the state's ability to impose and collect taxes in particular money-stuff (be it commodity, fiat paper, etc.).

We have jumped over some important stages in the evolution of money from debts. Even though capitalist credit-monies were means of payment

---

2. Wennerlind, "Money Talks," 557.
3. Ingham, "Fundamentals of a Theory," 311–12; italics in the original.

with no stable relationship to commodities, they did not become currency until debts became *fungible*. To turn to currency, debts and acceptance of "promises to pay" had to be detached from personality, persons, and organizations to become completely transferable. The transformation of the social relations between creditors and debtors, state and their creditors, into money took place gradually and evolved in tandem with the transformation of personal trust into impersonal trust, from accepting IOUs based on person-to-person (limited radius of trust) to an impersonal, generalizable trust anchored on the guarantee of the whole community.

A question suggests itself here: Is all money credit-money and what might have served as money before debts became detachable and alienable? When I argue that money is a social relation, I am not limiting the conception to only credit-money which is easy to grasp in an environment of institutionalized banking practice. I also maintain that archaic "commodity forms" of money could not have developed without social relations, and this is in at least two senses. First, every form of money needs a unit of account, abstract measure of value. Once exchange has developed beyond pure bilateral system into a complex multilateral system of multiple goods there has to be an abstract measure of value that may or may not be embodied in a commodity. And at this stage, that is, the stage that is beyond bilateral dealings between two persons or two sets of goods, all exchanges involve a third party. "The pivotal point in the interaction of the two parties recedes from direct line of contact between them, and moves to the relationship which each of them has with the economic community that accepts money."[4] The second sense of money's social relationality concerns the fact that even commodity-money like metallic money is a promise to pay and a claim. As Georg Simmel puts it:

> Metallic money is also a promise to pay and . . . it differs from the cheque only with respect to the size of the group which vouches for its being accepted. The common relationship that the owner of money and the seller have to a social group—the claim of the former to a service and the trust of the latter that this claim will be honoured—provides the sociological constellation in which money transactions, as distinct from barter are accomplished.[5]

If Simmel is correct (and I think he is) that all monies are credits, then the question is: Are all credits money? Money is not automatically created

---

4. Simmel, *Philosophy of Money*, 177.
5. Ibid., 178; see also 174–79 for whole argument that metallic money involves credit.

any time credits, promises/IOUs are generated. A credit only becomes money when the credit is socially accepted as money. Money is simultaneously a credit (asset) and debt (liability). So if a credit (debt) is created between any two economic agents and no third party wants to hold it as an asset it is not money. "Thus, it is more accurate to say that anyone can make promises or offer to go into debt but that the 'problem' is to find someone who is willing to become a creditor (i.e., to hold that "promise to pay" or debt)."[6]

Let me approach the argument from another perspective which will further establish the social relationality of money—*that of money as a claim*. In 1900 Georg Simmel seeing money as a form of *sociation*, constituted by the social relation of credit, posits that money is "only a claim upon society" and its realization depends upon "the community as a whole or upon the government as its representatives."[7] Simmel's analysis of economic value anticipated the Saussurian structuralist interpretation of value in the twentieth century. In reinterpreting the source of value and meaning of objects, he shifted scholarly focus from referentiality to relationality.[8] He avers:

> The economic value of objects is constituted by their mutual relationship and exchangeability. . . . The philosophical significance of money is that it represents within the practical world the most certain image and the clearest embodiment of the formula of all being, according to which things receive their meaning through each other, and have their being determined by their mutual relations.[9]

One hundred and five years after Simmel's claim theory of money, Bruce G. Carruthers in 2005 followed with this statement: "I define money as *generalized, immediate, and transferable legitimate claims on value.*

---

6. See Bell, "Role of the State," 151.

7. Simmel, *Philosophy of Money*, 177.

8. In spite of Simmel's profound analysis of money, it still suffers from three deficiencies. It lacks a discussion of how the abstract value of money is established and maintained. Besides, in his relational, subjective interplay of forces and preferences, which establish the value of commodities, money plays only a neutral role, as in the theories of the neoclassical economists. In the autopoietic (self-maintaining and self-referential) functioning of the valuation system, the social structure that stands behind price formation in Max Weber's economic struggle of "man against man" is ignored. Finally, Simmel somehow thinks that the abstract value of money depends on the process of dematerialization of money-stuff (Ibid., 191). This is an error many analysts still make today. The abstract unit of account precedes the concrete medium of exchange and it is not dependent on the abstraction (dematerialization) of money.

9. Ibid., 120, 128–29.

A Relational Theology of Money

Money is important because it commands resources. . . . Claims are general only within social communities and spheres of activity. . . . Finally, both claims and values to which they apply are socially constructed. What constitutes value in one society may be valueless in others."[10]

Once you accept the definition that money is a general claim on value, it follows easily or necessarily that it is a social relation. This point can be elaborated at three levels. First, social relation itself is a claim on value and thus money is only a form of social relations.[11] Second, from another angle it is to note that any general claim on resources within a given society is a social claim—"claims are general only within social communities and spheres of activity." Third, money is advantageous to an individual or any two agents if others use it. Once exchange transaction developed beyond the two-way arrangement of barter into mediation by money (with its intrinsic social nature as a promise) every exchange became a tripartite transaction. The money that a buyer hands over to a seller in exchange for a product is a claim on the future wealth of society. The piece of paper or metal is accepted by the seller because it will enable her to claim a piece of society's wealth just as the buyer has just done. Pixley adequately captures this promise-of-claim nature of money as supported by third party when she writes:

> In its "claim" dimension, money is not simply bipartisan, imprisoned in a single moment in the space between two people. It is a promise into the future, and as a token of that promise it can only be created between three parties. No one can believe or trust this token or promissory note unless it includes the "community that guarantees the money" . . . It is a three-way relation between the credit and debt relations of the economically active groups and the central power that enforces these promises by unifying and issuing a currency and outlawing counterfeiting.[12]

The argument so far lends itself to a quick summary so that we can tentatively capture what has been established so far. Money is a social relation of depersonalized, alienated, exchangeable promises. It is a packaged

---

10. Carruthers, "Sociology of Money and Credit," 355; italics in the original.

11. Social relation is a claim on value (economic and non-economic resources). The definition of social relation as claim on value indicates that it has a dimension of obligation. Every social relation seeks to draw and retain resources so that the individuals in it can perpetuate themselves into the future. For a fuller discussion of this point, see my *God and Money*, chap. 4.

12. Pixley, *Emotions in Finance*, 8.

(monetized) social relation of debt, an institutionalized set of promises between creditors and debtors, guaranteed by a community. The Australian sociologist Jocelyn Pixley in her book, *Emotions in Finance*, puts it this way: "The money in our wallets and purses is part of an abstract chain of social relations of claims and credits, no less organized than plastic card money and bank mortgages."[13]

It is germane to point out at this juncture that the key interest of all of the preceding discourse is *an attempt to locate social relations within money itself rather than seeing social relations as external to money or investigating how money is used to create and mark distinct social relations.*

When this last point is taken together in the light of the overall discussions of this chapter it should be noted that I am trying to make the overall assertion that money is social in two fundamental senses. First, it is to acknowledge that monetary transactions are embedded in social relations, to recognize how the monetization process is reshaping social practices or to understand how persons and groups negotiate the intersections of economic processes and social ties. Second is to note that social relations are constitutive of money. These two points amply show the overall social character of money.

What kind of theological resources can be brought to bear on crises and problems in the social practice of money? For instance, how can we interpret, evaluate, and aid the transformation of the monetary system in the light of the dynamic relations of the triune God? The Trinity is a communion of interdependent divine persons and the relations in it are not monocentric or bipolar but symmetrical. We need to draw on the practical consequences of the doctrine of the Trinity based on the perichoretic interpretation to show how the monetary system can be used to create an embracing economic community that brings *unity-in-difference* into perpetual play and justifies no "privileges, and no subjugations and submittances."[14]

Love is an essential attribute of this communion as 1 John 4:8 informs us. Thomas Jay Oord puts it well when he states: "It is necessarily the case that God [a relational being whose love is full-orbed] acts intentionally, in sympathetic response to others (which includes past divine actions), to promote overall well-being. Loving others is not an arbitrarily divine decision but rather an aspect of God's eternal, unchanging nature."[15] Oord goes

13. Ibid., 7.
14. Moltmann, *Coming Of God*, 183.
15. Oord, *Defining Love*, 189.

on to argue that the divine form of love, like creaturely love, also expresses itself as "*agape, eros,* and *philia,* and sometimes these forms mix."¹⁶

The ethical reasoning behind this turn to the triune God is that critique of the current monetary system can draw from these theologically conceived qualities of the Trinity to ground the exposition of the values, power differential, and the domination of the system that are threatening the moral order of our communities. For an understanding of the most developed Christian view of positive relations and relationships, the logical place to look is the trinitarian language of the Christian tradition. Besides, such knowledge of and commitment to positive relationships should inspire us to develop some ethical principles to guide the transformation of our financial systems in ways that can improve monetary relations between various economic classes in our communities.

The model of the dynamic relations of the triune God is also useful when applied to the issues of power differentials that are embedded in the current global monetary system. It is particularly so when it functions as an imaginative framework for crafting an inclusive, non-hierarchical alternative to any socio-economic system. I am interested in forging an alternative to the current structures of the monetary system because of my sense of justice. For me the praxis of justice in the national economy, and for that matter the world economy, is about drawing all nations, classes, and persons (poor and rich, powerful and not-so powerful) to share in a living communion by removing or challenging structures that thwart relationship of equality and participation.

Work and Monetary Policy

Earlier in chapter 4 we discussed the importance of the relationship between a society's conception of money, well-being, and economic flourishment. Before then we also argued that money—in the forms of credit economy, exchange, and capital—is the condition of possibility for work. Here we want to craft a theology of money around the issue of work and the role of monetary policy in promoting work. By focusing the theology of money on work I am attempting to accomplish three goals at once. First, expand the usual focus of theology of money beyond the limits of stewardship. Second, United States is in a period of high labor unemployment and it is important to show how a Christian theology of work can relate to this

16. Ibid., 190.

pressing human crisis. Finally, the expanded focus brings to the attention of ministerial leaders the importance of monetary policy in their struggles against poverty and social justice. Earlier generations of ministers and public leaders recognized the importance of monetary policies on the lives of ordinary folks. One example is the presidential campaign of William Jennings Bryant in 1896 when he gave his famous speech at the Democratic National Convention in Chicago about bimetallism or free silver: "you shall not crucify mankind upon a cross of gold." The struggles that led to the creation of the Federal Reserve Board with its original independent, decentralized regional representation were part of a wider campaign for economic and social justice.

Here I want to construct an alternative perspective from which the world of monetary policy is to be seen. The major reason in doing this is to show how monetary policy should be thought about and crafted to identify the true potentials of an economy, region, sector, or market situation to enable them to be realized. This imaginative framework is important to develop even if political and economic realities block its immediate implementation. The alternative thinking this framework provides, at the minimum, exposes the values of the current monetary-policy regime that are threatening the moral order of many a nation and thus serves as a critique of the current monetary thought that dominates development thinking. I am discussing monetary policy issues together with work because the primary goal of monetary policy is to order work aright in any economy.

Work is the unfurling of humanity toward a wholeness in which all selves and others are inextricably linked.[17] Work is the daily means (involving body, mind, and spirit) of humanity to begin, to cut open (*be-ginnan*) the iterative dynamic of becoming itself that is human existence. That a fresh beginning be made in the fluid dynamics of transcending our current humanity work is done. Working is fundamentally the communication and exchange of that by which a human being is in dynamism of positing a new possible world.[18] The *that* that is communicated is the set of possibilities (potentials) for forward movement. Work is that by which the human being "stand in" and "stand out" of actualization of potentialities, the processive openness toward the not-yet.

---

17. Wariboko, *Depth and Destiny of Work*, 4–14, 233–38.

18. I have reworked Albino Barrera's phrasing for my purpose here. See his *God and Evil*, 219.

The importance of monetary policy in producing the right environment for persons to triumph and prosper in their work cannot be overstated. Monetary policy is what orders work in any modern economy. Monetary policy is the mobilization of an economy's monetary and financial resources for the preservation, promotion, and ordering of its work. Productive and reproductive work—organization and distribution of rewards thereof—maintains the structure of mutuality of life through which a people shape their lives and cope with their day-to-day problems. The control of the money supply in any economy affects which work prospers and which work weakens in it; and so determines "who shall benefit and who shall sacrifice"[19] in the production and reproduction processes of life.

Every organization of monetary system, and for that matter, work, is coded with its own peculiar set of principles, motivations, and information for either supporting or thwarting (even if unwittingly) the actualization of human potentialities of all citizens. It is, therefore, important for us to spend some time reflecting on the approach to monetary policy that will foster economic development as an opportunity for and a process and product of increasing the range of actualization.

Everywhere, monetary policy shapes the landscape of economic and social lives. How it does this is dependent on a philosophical-ethical understanding of the role of monetary policy in modern economies. Is monetary policy simply a technical adjustment of quantities of money in an economy or sophistic manipulation of interest rates with no connections to deep national aspirations? Or is it rather suffused with discernment of entrepreneurial passions and highly ethical judgment as to what is of value and importance to the development of a national economy? I will argue that there can be no adequate ethical perspective on monetary policy without an adequate understanding of what I will call the *eros* of money.

The crucial role of monetary policy is to tap the wellspring of vital energies in the socioeconomic phenomenon that is money for economic growth and development. A good and development-oriented national monetary policy should offer the experience of both the fulfillment and endless awakening of the creative force and yearning for mutuality in the national economy. There is a connection-making power of money that a good monetary policy can unleash on society. A monetary policy is good, among other considerations, when it expresses possibilities for wider integration, cooperation, and transformation at both the personal and

---

19. Winter, *Community and Spiritual Transformation*, 104.

transpersonal levels in an economy. It is good when it can positively shape communal relationships. Additionally, from a nationalistic point of view it is good when citizens can see their own "spirit," values, ideals, and hopes incarnated in it.

Some neoclassical economists may consider the above ethical stance on monetary policy "strange." But the stance came after reflection on the received neoclassical economic wisdom on money and the need to transcend the limited perspective it offers. Those of us who are interested in liberating the poor from "unfreedoms" should learn to think new thoughts even as we think the thoughts of Milton Friedman and his cohorts. I am offering a "strange" perspective on monetary policy not out of a desire to stand outside the ballpark of mainstream monetary thinking, but to *un-conceal* a new vista in monetary-policy thinking. It is my hope that this vista may give us an opening for new possibilities in poor economies; to enable them move from lower levels of performance to the highest possible levels.

It does no good to only focus on the quantity of money in monetary-policy decisions as this is generally done in the leading central banks of the world. Money is not a mere quantitative thing. It is something that has the vitality to grow and expand, to connect and nourish all those persons and sectors it touches. It has the power to transform and deepen relationships between economic actors and their economy if properly handled.[20] It is this vitality, energy, impulse that I have named as the *eros* of money. *Eros* is the power of creativity, the impulse to move from a lower standing to a higher dimension, the transition from brokenness to wholeness. It is power in human sociality to secure that which is salient and essential to its well-being and greater flourishing.

It was Plato, in his *Symposium*, who put out the argument that there is an impulse in all beings to move from incompleteness to wholeness, to desire that which will complete them. This movement, the transitions to higher levels of fulfillment, he named as *eros*. The purpose of the movement or desire is not just for the sake of coming together, but it is to release the power of creativity in humanity for the sake of a flourishing life. *Eros* is a power that underlies all of human creativity, from procreation to the love of philosophical wisdom, he argued. Eros is a life-giving power and the driving force in all of human coexistence, including economic togetherness and cultural creativity. *Eros* is both an awareness and movement in the direction of greater flourishing. It is about a painful awareness of a gap and

---

20. See Wariboko, *God and Money*.

the desire to close that separateness, a demand to possess that which the person does not wholly possess. The sheer separateness from that which will make one whole releases one's vitality for the pursuit of wholeness and greatness necessary for happiness or *eudaimonia*.

The kinds of separateness and incompleteness that have been undermining economic development in the Majority World economies are not hard to discern. What has been hard to notice is a deliberate attempt to release the kind of *creative eros* that can raise them beyond poverty and underdevelopment. Incompleteness in their economies is revealed in their dependency, decades of failure to raise living standards, monetary systems that are not geared to development of internal resources, crippling urban and rural disarticulation, and massive income inequality that eviscerates the well-being of the poor. For too long, poor countries have been separated from the flourishing economies they should have. Everywhere their people look they experience the *pathos* of separation and poverty in their midst. All of these also apply to poor people and the poor regions in the United States.

Monetary policy then should both be a paradigm and a series of steps that aim to bring their longing and incompleteness to an end. Majority World's central bank should be aiming at releasing the creative and animating force that is in money so that it can exert positive influence in all spheres of their economies, connecting regions and sectors. Those charged with making their monetary policies need to make all good efforts to understand the "essential nature of money," not simply its twisted expressions under the conditions of underdevelopment, neocolonialism, and empire as we currently find all over Africa, Asia, and Latin America. The "essence" of money is its *creative eros*. The *telos* of developing economies' central banks should be to remove the cleavage between the "essence" of money and its twisted and ambiguous expressions in their countries; to overcome the chasm between their potentialities and current levels of achievement, to encourage every economic agent to strive and yearn to raise him or herself toward higher levels. Monetary policy should be a source of movement of the citizens toward integrated, internally-powered development.

In order for us to understand how monetary policy can be a source of movement toward a well-articulated economy, we need to decipher the elements of *eros* and lift them up as norms of monetary policy. The hope is that the pursuit of these norms in decision-making by central banks will fruitfully enable poor economies to resist underdevelopment (a kind of *nonbeing*) and preserve and promote development (*being*).

Following Paul Tillich, I interpret *eros* as the umbrella Greek word for love with four components: *epithymia, philia, eros,* ag*ape*.[21] *Epythymia* (longing) names the desire to fulfill need. Simply, it is the recognition of a need and the movement to satisfy the need. This word in Latin is *libido* and in the hands of Freud it came to stand for unlimited sexual desire, the desire for pleasure through another being, and thus acquired a very bad name. In the old sense, *epithymia* refers, for example, to hunger for knowledge, food, power, material wealth, spiritual values, sex, and participation in group. It referred to the thirst and hunger in all human praxis in which needy persons move toward the objects that fulfill their needs. The focus is not on pleasure, but that which fulfills one's desire. Freud is wrong to reduce it to a pain-pleasure principle. *Philia* is the movement toward union between equals, working cooperatively. The part within *eros* that bears its name points to a movement of that which is lower in a scale of value toward that which is higher, enhancing value. *Agape* is the part of love that affirms the other unconditionally; it affirms not because the other is higher or lower, pleasant or unpleasant, desirable or undesirable. The only interest is to draw the other into a union, to promote overall well-being. When *agape* is present in a relationship, it can transform and purify the other components of love and move them to their pure forms as dynamic movements of the separated (estranged) to union.

The Platonic-Greek philosophical idea of love as *eros* is not about pleasurable feeling, but a creative, dynamic, primal power that moves the world toward fulfillment and deepens relationships. It is the connection-making power in human life and the whole of the universe. Money is a form of *eros* in any modern economy because it is the moving power of economic life. Money is not a mere tool of exchange; it is a force (a form of social relation[22]) that calls persons, regions, and sectors beyond themselves and draws them from separation, detachment, and disarticulation into integration, articulation, and participation in the unfolding creative processes of an economy.

Money is actually a two-edged sword. Money connects, money separates. It cuts and attaches. Money looks inwards and outwards. It is both constructive and destructive. The *creative eros* of money reveals the

---

21. My analysis is drawn from Tillich, *Love, Power, and Justice*, 25–34, 116.
22. See Wariboko, *God and Money*, chap. 4.

A Relational Theology of Money

constructive power of money over its negation. Money embraces within itself destructive forces that are opposed to its *creative eros*. When we speak of the *creative eros* of money, it is only with an affirmation of money's positive constructive force in recognition of its destructive potentials. Monetary policy is, simply, an affirmation of money's creative forces while resisting its destructive tendencies. The real expertise in central banking is to acquire and preserve the power to affirm the creative forces of money in spite of the destructive ones over and over again.

This is one of the ways central bankers can affirm the *creative eros* of money through policy. They set and abide by some basic norms that can induce and sustain relationality, mutuality, and transition to higher levels of economic performance and human flourishing in their economies. The norms come from adapting and transforming Tillich's elements of love into a set of ethical canons for monetary policy. First, the criterion of *stimulation (epithymia)* is the capacity of monetary policy to drive economic agents into more and more intercourse and interdependence, to stimulate the movement of the less vibrant, less efficient sectors and agents toward sectors, areas, and resource centers that fulfill them. In order to promote economic interdependence and eliminate all forms of insidious economic duality, monetary policies must encourage the movement of the deficit (that is, needful, less vibrant, less efficient, less articulated) industries toward the sectors and resource centers that will help to liberate their potentials and fulfill them.

The second norm is about the criterion of *integration (philia)*. Monetary policy should not only stimulate intersectoral intercourse but also encourage and sustain movement toward better integration and union within each sector and region. While *stimulation* is an external movement of sectors, *integration* is about internal movement within sectors and regions. Monetary and fiscal policies must encourage movement toward better integration and union within each sector and region. In terms of persons, this involves providing equality of access to the present and accumulated economic and social resources so that most persons will have equal opportunity to develop their capabilities and fully participate in the preservation and promotion of their community well-being.

The third norm is *transformative*. Monetary policy should promote right relationship, pushing or pulling all sectors, industries, regions, and persons from levels lower in cooperativeness and possibilities toward their highest forms. The fourth norm is that of *promotion of sociality* inherent in the social practice of work. The issue is how to know whether a certain monetary-policy regime is structured to include all groups and classes to participate fully in the economy so as to create flourishing lives for themselves or not. Does it foster participation and communion, human mutuality, and reciprocity? The right monetary policy that fosters participation and communion points to an *eros* quality in every interpersonal and intersectoral relation in the economy. Mutuality is the key category for understanding the nature of money, work, and monetary policy. Mutuality is also the central symbol as well as the source of norms. The accent of mutuality is on comprehensive inclusiveness; that is, to include all groups, classes, sectors, and regions to participate fully in the economy so as to create flourishing lives for themselves.

The knowledge of how to generate and sustain the *creative eros* of money is the mother of all forms of monetary knowledge. This knowledge is about initiating and sustaining collective capacity, knowing how to integrate sectors, discerning how to harness the dispersed energies of the citizens to the goal of national flourishing, how to marshal individual economic resources to act on the common good, and how to orient all men and women toward excellence.[23]

This concern or focus of monetary policy shows openness to the triune relationality. The significance of monetary policy is nurturing, fostering the social practices of money to approximate the mutuality of the Godhead. An ethical monetary policy, as we have argued, is about the continuous proper ordering and balancing of economic powers (potentialities) in community or communities to sustain harmonious relationships, reduce injustice, and acknowledge the worth of all persons. The ultimate meaning of monetary policy is its capacity to point to the trinitarian communion even as it helps to create an embracing community.

---

23. Excellence is about enabling each and every member of society to realize his or her potentialities. It involves creating the environment for each person to become all that he or she can be.

Bibliography

Abram, David. *The Spell of the Sensuous*. New York: Vintage Books, 1996.
Adams, Roberts Merrihew. *A Theory of Virtue: Excellence in Being for the Good*. Oxford: Oxford University Press, 2006.
Agamben, Giorgio. *Profanation*. Translated by Jeff Fort. New York: Zone Books, 2007.
Alesina, Alberto, Rafael di Tella, and Robert MacCulloch. "Inequality and Happiness: Are Europeans and Americans Different?" *National Bureau of Economic Research Working Paper* 8198. Cambridge, MA, April 2001.
Altvater, Elmar. "The Foundations of Life (Nature) and the Maintenance of Life (Work)." *International Journal of Political Economy* 20 (1990) 10–34.
Alvey, James. "Lisa Hill's Discovery of Adam Smith's 'Hidden Theology,'" Paper presented at the *Australian Political Studies Association Conference*, University of Adelaide, Adelaide, September 29 to October 1, 2004.
Aristotle. *Politics*. In *The Basic Works of Aristotle*, edited and introduced by Richard Mckeon, 1127–1316. New York: Random, 1941.
Awe, David O. *Accounting, Compliance, and Tax Guide for Churches and Ministers*. Publishing location unknown: Deleawe Publications, 2010.
Badiou, Alain. *Being and Event*. Translated by Oliver Feltham. London: Continuum, 2005.
Barrera, Albino. *God and Evil of Scarcity: Moral Foundations of Economic Agency*. Notre Dame: University of Notre Dame Press, 2005.
Bauman, Zygmunt. *Postmodern Ethics*. Oxford: Blackwell, 1994.
Bell, Stephanie. "The Role of the State and the Hierarchy of Money." *Cambridge Journal of Economics* 25, no. 3 (2001) 149–63.
Bellah, Robert N. *Beyond Belief: Essay in Religion in a Post-Traditional World*. New York: Harper & Row, 1970.
Bernstein, Peter L. *Against the Gods: The Remarkable Story of Risk*. New York: John Wiley & Sons, 1996.
Bonk, Jonathan J. *Missions and Money: Affluence as a Missionary Problem . . . Revisited*. Maryknoll, NY: Orbis, 2011.
Born, Daniel. *The Birth of Liberal Guilt in the English Novel: Charles Dickens to H. G. Wells*. Chapel Hill: University of North Carolina Press, 1995.
Bruce, Steve. *God is Dead: Secularization in the West*. Malden, MA: Blackwell, 2002.
Buber, Martin. *I and Thou*. New York: Scribner, 1958.
Bühlmann, Walbert. Foreword to *Missions and Money: Affluence as a Missionary Problem . . . Revisited*, by Jonathan J. Bonk, xi–xvi. Maryknoll, NY: Orbis, 2011.
Caputo, John D. *Against Ethics*. Bloomington: Indiana University Press, 1993.
———. *Deconstruction in a Nutshell: A Conversation with Jacques Derrida*. New York: Fordham University Press, 1997.

Bibliography

Carruthers, Bruce. "The Sociology of Money and Credit." In *The Handbook of Economic Sociology*, 2nd ed., edited by N. J. Smelser and R. Swedberg, 355–78. Princeton: Princeton University Press, 2005.

Cowen, Tyler, and Randall Kroszner. *Explorations in the New Monetary Economics*. Cambridge: Blackwell, 1994.

Cullman, Oscar, Harry A. Wolfson, Werner Jaeger, and Henry J. Cadbury. *Immortality and Resurrection: Death in the Western World: Two Conflicting Currents of Thought*. New York: Macmillan, 1965.

Cunningham, David S. "Participation as Trinitarian Virtue: Challenging the Current 'Relational' Consensus." *Toronto Journal of Theology* 14, no. 1 (1998) 7–25.

Derrida, Jacques. *Dissemination*. Translated by Barbara Johnson. London: Athlone, 1981.

———. *The Gift of Death and Literature in Secret*. Translated by David Wills. Chicago: University of Chicago Press, 2008.

Dickens, Charles. *Little Dorrit*. Harmondsworth: Penguin, 1857.

Diulio, Eugene A. *Theory and Problems of Macroeconomic Theory*. New York: McGraw-Hill, 1990.

Dodd, Nigel. "Reinventing Monies in Europe." *Economy and Society* 34, no. 4 (November 2005) 558–83.

Drummond, Sarah. *Holy Clarity: The Practice of Planning and Evaluation*. Herndon, VA: Alban Institute, 2009.

Dumont, Louis. *Essays on Individualism: Modern Ideology in Anthropological Perspective*. Chicago: University of Chicago Press, 1986.

Eaglestone, Robert. *Ethical Criticism: Reading after Levinas*. Edinburgh: University of Edinburgh Press, 1997.

Ekelund, Robert B., Robert F. Hebert, Robert D. Tollison, Gary Anderson, and Audrey B. Davidson. *Sacred Trust: The Medieval Church as an Economic Firm*. New York: Oxford University Press, 1996.

Evangelical Council for Financial Accountability. "ECFA Standard 5—Transparency." Online: http://www.ecfa.org/content/comment5. Accessed May 12, 2012.

Foucault, Michael. *Power/Knowledge: Selected Interviews and Other Writings 1972–1977*. Edited by Colin Gordon. Translated by Colin Gordon et al. New York: Pantheon, 1980.

Friedman, Benjamin M. *The Moral Consequences of Economic Growth*. New York: Knopf, 2005.

Fukuyama, Francis. *Trust: The Social Virtues and the Creation of Prosperity*. New York: Free Press, 1995.

Ganssman, Heiner. "Book Review: Geoffrey Ingham, 'The Nature of Money.'" *Economic Sociology, European Electronic Newsletter* 6, no.1 (October 2004) 29–32.

Goodchild, Philip. "Capital and Kingdom: An Eschatological Ontology." In *Theology and the Political: The New Debate*, edited by Creston Davies, John Milbank, and Slavoj Zizek, 127–52. Durham, NC: Duke University Press, 2005.

Gregersen, Niels Henrik. "Faith in a World of Risks: A Trinitarian Theology of Risk-Taking." In *For All People: Global Theologies in Contexts*, edited by Else Marie Wiberg Pedersen, Holgar Lam, and Peter Lodberg, 214–33. Grand Rapids: Eerdmans, 2002.

———. "Risk and Religion: Toward a Theology of Risk Taking." *Zygon* 38, no. 2 (June 2003) 355–76.

Gregory, Christopher A. *Gifts and Commodities*. London: Academic, 1982.

Gunton, Colin E. *Father, Son and Holy Spirit: Toward a Fully Trinitarian Theology*. London: T. & T. Clark, 2003.
Hallward, Peter. *Badiou: A Subject to Truth*. Minneapolis: University of Minnesota Press, 2003.
Hart, Kelvin. *Money in an Unequal World: Keith Hart and His Memory Bank*. London: Texere, 2000.
Hauerwas, Stanley. *A Community of Character: Toward a Constructive Christian Social Ethic* Notre Dame: University of Notre Dame Press, 1981.
Hill, Lisa. "The Hidden Theology of Adam Smith." *European Journal of the History of Economic Thought* 8, no. 1 (2001) 1–29.
Hirschman, Albert O. *The Passions and the Interest: Political Arguments for Capitalism before Its Triumph*. Princeton: Princeton University Press, 1977.
Ingham, Geoffrey. "Fundamentals of a Theory of Money: Untangling Fine, Lapavitsas and Zelizer." *Economy and Society* 30, no. 3 (2001) 304–23.
Internal Revenue Service. "Intermediate Sanctions—Excess Benefit Transactions." Online: http://www.irs.gov/Charities-&-Non-Profits/Charitable-Organizations/Intermediate-Sanctions-Excess-Benefit-Transactions. Accessed May 13, 2012.
———. "Internal Revenue Bulletin: 2005–24." Online: http://www.irs.gov/irb/2005-24_IRB/ar13.html. Accessed May 13, 2012.
———. *Tax Guide for Churches and Religious Organizations*. Online: http://www.irs.gov/pub/irs-pdf/p1828.pdf. Accessed May 14, 2012.
James, Robison B. "Historicizing God àla Tillich and Barth (Both!): Formula for Good Theology." *North American Paul Tillich Society* 37, no. 1 (Winter 2011) 10–18.
Jamieson, Janet T., and Philip D. Jamieson. *Ministry and Money: A Practical Guide for Pastors*. Louisville, KY: Westminster John Knox, 2009.
Kohák, Erazim. *Jan Patočka: Philosophy and Selected Writings*. Chicago: University of Chicago Press, 1989.
Landes, David S. *Revolution in Time*. Cambridge: Harvard University Press, 1983.
———. *The Wealth and Poverty of Nations: Why Some are So Rich and Some So Poor*. New York: W. W. Norton, 1998.
Lind, R. C. "A Primer on the Major Issues Relating to the Discount Rate for Evaluating Energy Options." In *Discounting for Time and Risk in Energy Policy*, edited by R. C. Lind et al, 21–114. Washington, DC: Resources for the Future, 1982.
Liu, Henry C. K. "More on the US Experience." *Asia Times Online*, November 27, 2002. Online: http://www.atimes.com/atimes/printN.html. Accessed June 21, 2005.
MacIntyre, Alasdair. *After Virtue*. Notre Dame: University of Notre Dame Press, 1984.
Madsen, Richard. *Morality and Power in a Chinese Village*. Berkeley: University of California Press, 1984.
Marx, Karl. *Grundrisse*. New York: Vintage, 1973.
———. "The Power of Money in Bourgeois Society." In *The Economic and Philosophical Manuscript of* 1844, 136–41. Moscow: Foreign Language, 1956.
Mishkin, Frederic S. *The Economics of Money, Banking, and Financial Markets*. Glenview, IL: Scott, Foresman, 1989.
Moltmann, Jürgen. *The Coming Of God: Christian Eschatology*. Translated by Margaret Kohl. Minneapolis: Fortress, 1996.
Nancy, Jean-Luc. *Dis-Enclosure: The Deconstruction of Christianity*. Translated by Bettina Bergo, Gabriel Malenfant, and Michael B. Smith. New York: Fordham University Press, 2008.

Bibliography

Nelson, Robert H. *Economics as Religion from Samuelson to Chicago and Beyond.* University Park: Pennsylvania State University Press, 2001.

———. *Reaching for Heaven on Earth: The Theological Meaning of Economics.* Savage, MD: Rowman & Littlefield, 1991.

Nelson, Benjamin N. *The Idea of Usury: From Tribal Brotherhood to Universal Otherhood.* Princeton: Princeton University Press, 1949.

———. "On Taking of Interest." In *On Moral Business: Classical and Contemporary Resources for Ethics in Economic Life*, edited by Max L. Stackhouse, Dennis P. McCann, Shirley J. Roels, and Preston N. Williams, 265–71. Grand Rapids: Eerdmans, 1995.

Niebuhr, Richard. *Christ and Culture.* New York: Harper Perennial, 1951.

Nietzsche, Friedrich. "The Genealogy of Morals." In *The Birth of Tragedy* and *The Genealogy of Morals*, translated by Francis Golffing, 147–299. Garden City, NY: Doubleday, 1956.

Nussbaum, Martha. *Sex and Social Justice.* Oxford: Oxford University Press, 1999.

———. *Upheavals in Thought: The Intelligence of Emotion.* Cambridge: Cambridge University Press, 2001.

Oord, Thomas Jay. *Defining Love: A Philosophical, Scientific, and Theological Engagement.* Grand Rapids: Brazos, 2010.

Oslington, Paul. "Natural Theology as an Integrative Framework." St. Marks Day Public Lecture, *St. Marks National Theological Center*, May 2005.

Pannenberg, Wolfhart. "The God of Hope." In *Basic Questions in Theology*, vol. 2, translated by George H. Kehm, 234–49. London: SCM, 1971.

Patočka, Jan. *Plato and Europe.* Translated by Petr Lom. Stanford: Stanford University Press, 2002.

Piper, Otto A. "That Strange Thing Money." *Theology Today* 6, no.2 (July 1959) 215–31.

Pixley, Jocelyn. *Emotions in Finance: Distrust and Uncertainty in Global Finance.* Cambridge: Cambridge University Press, 2004.

Royce, Josiah. *The Problem of Christianity.* Washington, DC: Catholic University of America Press, 2001[1913].

Sacks, Jonathan. *The Dignity of Difference: How to Avoid the Clash of Civilization.* London: Continuum, 2003.

Samuelson, Paul. *Economics.* 9th ed. New York: McGraw-Hill, 1973.

Sandel, Michael J. *What Money Can't Buy: The Moral Limits of Markets.* New York: Farrar, Straus, and Giroux, 2012.

Sanneh, Lamin. *Translating the Message: The Missionary Impact on Culture.* 2nd ed. Maryknoll: Orbis, 2009.

Schumpeter, Joseph A. *History of Economic Analysis.* New York: Oxford University Press, 1954.

Schwöbel, Christoph, and Colin E. Gunton. *Persons, Divine and Human: King's College Essays in Theological Anthropology.* Edinburgh: T. & T. Clark, 1991.

Searle, John R. "Social Ontology and Political Power." Online: www.law.berkeley.edu/centers/kadish/searle.pdf. Accessed July 26, 2006.

Serequeberhan, Tsenay. *The Hermeneutics of African Philosophy: Horizon and Discourse.* New York: Routledge, 1994.

Sharp, Clifford. *The Economics of Time.* Oxford: Martin Robertson, 1981.

Shubik, Martin. *The Theory of Money and Financial Institutions.* Vol. 1. Cambridge: MIT Press, 1997.

Bibliography

Simmel, Georg. *The Philosophy of Money*. Translated by Tom Bottomore and David Frisby. New York: Routledge, 1978.
Smith, Adam. *The Theory of Moral Sentiments*. Edited by D. D. Raphael and A. L. Macfie. Oxford: Clarendon Press, 1976.
———. *The Wealth of Nations*. New York: Modern Library, 2000.
Stackhouse, Max L. *Ethics and the Urban Ethos: An Essay in Social Theory and Theological Reconstruction*. Boston: Beacon, 1972.
———. Introduction to *God and Globalization: Volume 1: Religion and the Powers of the Common Life*, edited by Max L. Stackhouse, with Peter Paris. Harrisburg, PA: Trinity, 2000.
———. Introduction to *God and Globalization: Volume 2: The Spirit and the Modern Authorities*, edited by Max L. Stackhouse, with Don S. Browning. Harrisburg, PA: Trinity, 2001.
———. "The Moral Roots of the Corporation." *Theology and Public Policy* 5, no. 1 (Summer 1993) 34.
———. *Public Theology and Political Economy: Christian Stewardship in Modern Society*. Lanham: University Press of America, 1991.
Stark, Rodney. *The Victory of Reason: How Christianity Led to Freedom, Capitalism, and Western Success*. New York: Random, 2005.
Stout, Jeffrey. *Ethics After Babel: The Languages of Morals and their Discontents*. Boston: Beacon, 1988.
Sutcliffe, Bob. "Development After Ecology." In *From Modernization to Globalization: Perspectives on Development and Social Change*, edited by T. Roberts and A. Hite, 328–39. Oxford, UK: Blackwell, 1995.
Tanner, Kathryn. *Economy of Grace*. Minneapolis: Fortress, 2005.
Taylor, Mark C. *Confidence Games: Money and Markets in a World Without Redemption* Chicago: University of Chicago Press, 2004.
Tillich, Paul. "The Importance of New Being for Christian Theology." In *Man and Transformation: Papers from the Eranos Yearbook* 30, no. 5, edited by Joseph Campbell, 161–78. New York: Bollingen Foundation, 1964.
———. *Love, Power, and Justice: Ontological Analyses and Ethical Applications*. London: Oxford University Press, 1954.
———. *The Protestant Era*. Chicago: University of Chicago Press, 1957.
———. *The Socialist Decision*. Translated by Franklin Sherman. New York: Harper & Row, [1933] 1977).
———. *Systematic Theology: Existence and the Christ, Volume 2*. Chicago: University of Chicago Press, 1957.
———. *Systematic Theology: Reason and Revelation, Being and God, Volume 1*. Chicago: University of Chicago Press, 1951.
Ulfers, Friedrich, and Mark Daniel Cohen. "Friedrich Nietzsche as Bridge from Nineteenth-Century Atomistic Science to Process Philosophy in Twentieth-Century Physics, Literature, and Ethics." *West Virginia University Philological Papers* 49 (2002) 21–29.
Volf, Miroslav. *Exclusion and Embrace: A Theological Exploration of Identity, Otherness, and Reconciliation*. Nashville: Abingdon, 1996.
———. *Free of Charge: Giving and Forgiving in a Culture Stripped of Grace*. Grand Rapids: Zondervan, 2005.
———. *Work in the Spirit: Toward a Theology of Work*. Eugene, OR: Wipf and Stock, 1991.

Bibliography

Wariboko, Nimi. *The Depth and Destiny of Work: An African Theological Interpretation*. Trenton, NJ: Africa World, 2008.

———. *Ethics and Time: Ethos of Temporal Orientation in Politics and Religion of the Niger Delta*. Lanham: Lexington, 2010.

———. *God and Money: A Theology of Money in a Globalizing World*. Lanham: Lexington, 2008.

———. *The Principle of Excellence: A Framework for Social Ethics*. Lanham: Lexington, 2009.

Waterman, Anthony M. C. "Economics as Theology: Adam Smith's *Wealth of Nations*." *Southern Economic Journal* 68, no. 4 (2002) 673–86.

———. *Political Economy and Christian Theology Since the Enlightenment*. New York: Palgrave Macmillan, 2004.

Weber, Max. *Economy and Society*. Berkeley: University of California Press, 1978.

———. "Religious Rejections of the World and their Directions." In *From Max Weber: Essays in Sociology*, edited by H. H. Gerth and C. W. Mills, 323–59. New York: Oxford University Press, 1958.

Wennerlind, Carl. "Money Talks, but What is it Saying? Semiotics of Money and Social Control." *Journal of Economic Issues* 35, no. 3 (September 2001) 557–69.

Williamson, Oliver. *The Economic Institutions of Capitalism*. New York: Free Press, 1985.

Wimberly, John W. Jr. *The Business of the Church: The Uncomfortable Truth that Faithful Ministry Requires Effective Management*. Herndon, VA: Alban Institute, 2010.

Winter, Gibson. *Community and Spiritual Transformation: Religion and Politics in a Communal Age*. New York: Crossroad, 1989.

Wolf, Martin. *Why Globalization Works*. New Haven: Yale University Press, 2004.

Woods, Thomas E. *The Church and the Market: A Catholic Defense of the Free Economy*. Latham: Lexington, 2005.

———. *How the Catholic Church Built Western Civilization*. Washington, DC: Regnery, 2005.

Yeats, William Butler. "The Second Coming." In *The Collected Poems of W. B. Yeats*, 211. London: MacMillan, 1933.

Zelizer, Viviana. "Circuits within Capitalism." In *The Economic Sociology of Capitalism*, edited by Victor Nee and Richard Swedberg, 289–322. Princeton: Princeton University Press, 2005.

———. "Human Values and the Market: The Case of Life Insurance and Death in 19th-Century America." *American Journal of Sociology* 84 (1978) 591–610.

———. "Payments and Social Ties." *Sociological Forum* 11 (September 1996) 481–95.

———. *The Purchase of Intimacy*. Princeton: Princeton University Press, 2005.

———. *The Social Meaning of Money: Pin Money, Paychecks, Poor Relief, and Other Currencies*. New York: Basic, 1994.

———. "Sociology of Money." In *International Encyclopedia of the Social and Behavioral Sciences* 15, edited by Neil J. Smelser and Paul B. Bates, 1991–94. Amsterdam: Elsevier, 2001.

Žižek, Slavoj. *Less than Nothing: Hegel and the Shadow of Dialectical Materialism*. London: Verso, 2012.

Subject Index

A

Abraham, 128
Abram, David, 28n14, 29n16, 29n17
accounting
    accrual accounting, 16
    and grace, 131–132
    and guilt, 92, 125, 130
    arithmetic foundation of equality, 122
    as a story, 14–15
    as narrative, 14–15
    as moral thought, 93
    binary opposition, 119, 136
    cash accounting, 16
    double entry, 16, 40, 119, 123, 130, 137, 139
    footnotes, 18, 21
    fundamental equation, xviii, 98, 123, 132–134, 140, 141
    ground norm of, 125, 126, 139, 140
    methods of, 16, 119, 136
    philosophy of, 124, 130, 133
accounting principles
    conservatism, 16
    consistency, 16
    cost concept, 17
    GAAP (generally accepted accounting principles), xvi, 20, 50, 126
    going concern, 17, 123
    matching, 16, 129, 135
    materiality, 17
    period, 17, 41
    recognition (revenue and expense), 16
action, 3, 57, 60, 137
actualization, 59, 60, 137, 138, 150, 151

actuarial science, 117
Africa, 153
Agamben, Giorgio, 91
Alesina, Alberto, 12
alterity, 98
Altvater, Elmar, 27, 29
Anaximander, 132
Aquinas, Thomas, 112
arche, 93, 99, 123
Arendt, Hannah, 57, 60
Argonauts, 85
Aristotle, 115
Arnauld, Antoine, 117
Asia, 153
Atlantic Ocean, 113
atonement, 92
attestation, 126
Augustine of Hippo, 104, 105
Awe, David O. 80
Azpilcueta, Martin de, 112

B

Badiou, Alain, 136n23, 137
bankers, 2, 10, 11, 12, 106, 108, 155
Bayes, Thomas, 117
Bayesian system, 117
be-ginnan, 150
Beecher, Henry Ward, 116
being-in-communion, xvi, 53, 95. See also communion and personhood
Bernstein, Peter, 110
Bible, 103
    Deuteronomy, 119
    Ephesians, 128
    Genesis, 103

163

Subject Index

Bible-continued
   I John, 148
   John, 114
   Mark, 70–71
   Matthew, 114
   Numbers, 102
binary opposition. See accounting
bondholder, 47
Bonk, Jonathan, 85
Born, Daniel, 125
Brand name, 4.
Britain, 103, 125
Bruce, Steve, 107
Buber, Martin, 95
budget, xvi, xvii, see also chapter 5
   and theology, 66
   as dead gaze, 75
   common-size adjustment technique, 68
   incremental budgeting, 67
   pro-forma analysis, 67
   theory of, 68, 69
   zero-based budgeting, 67
Bryant, Jennings William, 150

C

calculability, 131
calling, 108, 109
Calvin, John, 103, 104, 119
capabilities, 52, 57, 61, 70, 96, 155
capital, 5, 28, 75, 112–113, 120, 149
   cost of, 26
   natural capital, 27–28
capricious man, 95
Caputo, John D., 129
Cardinal Cajetan, 106
Cardinal Juan de Lugo, 106
care of the soul, 3, 73
Carruthers, Bruce G., 146
cash flows, 17, 20, 39, 44–47, 78
central banking, 9n3, 10, 12, 12n12, 138,142, 152–153, 155. See also Federal Reserve Board
ceremonies of innocence, 11
chief executive officer
   pastor as, xii, xiii, xiv, 2
China, 102
Chios, 115
Christ and Culture, xv, 36–37
Church
   and political campaign, 33
   definition by IRS, 31–32
   ecology of the church, 3, 14
   elements of the church, 3–4
class struggle, 10, 62
Clennam, Arthur, 125. See also Charles Dickens
coincidence of opposites, 120
coinherence, 64
commercial banks, 25, 26, 142
common good, 57, 59, 156
Commonwealth, 104
communal brotherhood, 118
communication, 68, 77, 140, 150
communion, xix, 15, 53–54, 62, 73, 95–97, 148–149, 156
compassion 69, 71, 73
compliance, xvii–xviii, 90–92, 94
condition of indifference, 137
Congress, 11
conscientious religious objection, 34
contingency, 113–114, 123
coroner, 135
corporate charter, 32
corporate ethics, 92
counted-as-one, 136, 137
coupon rate, 111
creative eros, 153, 154, 155, 156. See also eros
credo, 121
cross of gold, 10, 150

D

Davies, Natalie, 127
dead gaze, 75
De Cambiis, 106
De Molina, Luis, 106
De Vio, Thomas, 106
debt, 47, 49, 130, 131. See also money
debtors' prison, 125

Subject Index

decision theory, 117
Derrida, Jacques, 124, 129, 131
Descartes, 29
development
    economic, 29–30, 55–64, 70–72, 75, 150–151, 153–154. See also economic growth
diastêma, 65
Dickens, Charles, 125
dignity, 59, 73, 102, 103
dike, 132
divine cunning, 120
divine favor, 103
divine judgment, 103
double entry, See accounting
Drummond, Sarah, 76
Dumont, Louis, 103

E

earmark, 23, 24, 51
economic growth, 9, 26–27, 151. See also development
economism, 95. See also neoclassical economics
egalitarianism, 102
Elisha, 72
Emotions in Finance, 148
environmental pollution, xv, 25–30. See also money
    and Western thought, 28–30
environmental sustainability, 26–29
epi-reading, 124
epistemological indeterminacy, 134
equilibrium, 104–105, 123, 131
eros, 51–53, 149, 152–156
eschatological orientations, 112
eschaton, 65
Essays Towards Solving A Problem in the Doctrine of Chances, 117
ethical scorekeeping, 130, 139
etymology, 91
eudaimonia, 58, 108, 153
Evangelical Council for Financial Accountability (ECFA), 79

excellence, xvii, 36, 52n2, 57, 58, 83, 156. See also virtues
excess benefit, 88–89
excess of parts, 136n25, 137
expectation theory, 106
externalities, 27

F

Fates, 110
Federal Reserve Board, 10–12, 25, 142, 150
feeding of the five thousand, 69–73
fiduciary responsibility, 81, 87, 118
financial analyst, 8, 47, 124
financial innovation, 137
financial product, 118, 137
Financial Times, 10
financialism, 63
fixed idée, 27
Florence, 144
flows of money, 73–74
foreign exchange market, 106
Foucault, Michel, 140n29
France, 117
franchise recognition, 4
Franklin, Benjamin, 117
freedom, 54, 57–58, 60, 103, 114, 123, 129
Freud, 154
Friedman, Benjamin M., 103
Friedman, Milton, 152
Fukuyama, Francis, 107, 109
fulfillment, 37, 56, 60, 151, 152, 154
future contracts, 115–116

G

game of chance, 117
Genealogy of Morals, 130
general equivalent of value, 135
generosity, 74, 129
Genoa, 144
gift, 113–114, 123, 127–128, 129, 140
Gift of Death, 131

165

Subject Index

global financial system, 100–101, 108, 115, 119, 120
God and Money: A Theology of Money in a Globalizing World, 25n11, 57n2, 61, 143, 147n11
God, Spirit of, 63, 68
Godhead, xix, 54, 62, 156. See also Trinity
Goodchild, Philip, 113
goods external, xvii, 36, 83–84
goods internal, xvii, 36, 83–84
Gospel, 35, 37, 66, 69, 119, 127
government securities, 25, 26, 142
grace, 85, 103, 123, 127, 131–132
Greek mythology, 84
Greeks, 85, 110, 113, 132, 133, 154
Gregersen, Neil Henrik, 113, 114
Gross National Product (GNP), 17, 27
ground norm, 125, 126, 139, 140. See also accounting
guilt, 92, 125, 130. See also accounting
Hauerwas, Stanley, 15n1
Hegel, 28, 120, 133
Heidegger, Martin, 29
heritage, 100, 103, 106, 107, 121
hermeneutical decoding, 124
Hill, Lisa, 105
Hirschman, Albert O. 104, 105, 105
history, 4, 15, 28, 60–61, 100, 116, 119, 121
Hobbes, Thomas, 28
Holy Clarity, 76, 77, 78
homo economicus, xviii, 94–954, 97
housing allowance, 35
hurricanes, 110, 113

I

idolatry, 52
imago Dei, 61, 97
inclusiveness, xix, 97, 156
individualism, 28, 101–103, 109
inflation, 10, 11, 17, 22, 62
Ingham, Geoffrey, 144
injustice, 10, 132, 138, 156
insider information, 128

insurance companies, 110
interest theory, 117
internal control, see chapter 6
philosophy of, 83–85
principles of, 80–82
inurement, 90
invisible hand, 64, 101, 104–106
IRS forms, 86–87
Isaac, 128

J

James, Robison, B., 61
Jansenist, 106
jar of oil, 72
Jason, 84, 85
Jastrow, Joseph, 74
Jesus Christ, xvi, 7, 37, 59–61, 64, 66, 69, 71, 72, 73, 115. See also Messiah and New Being
Judeo-Christian ethos, 100, 120
Kierkegaard, 129
kingdom of God, xi, xii, 37, 53, 77
Kuyper, Abraham, 51
Laborem Excerens, 108
Landes, David, 102, 111
Latin America, 153
legal tender, 142, 144
Lessines, Giles, 112
levels of movement, 2–3
    acceptance, 2–3
    defense, 2–3
    transformation, 2–3
Levinas, Emmanuel, 131
life insurance, 116, 117, 130
liquidity ratio, 47
Little Dorrit, 125
loaves and fish, 69, 71. See also feeding of the five thousand
London, 10, 109, 125
lordship and bondage, 28
love, 104, 105, 106, 114, 148, 149, 152
    and monetary policy, 152–156
    as *agape*, 149, 154
    as *epithymia*, 154, 155
    as *eros*, 149, 154. See also *eros*.

Subject Index

as *libido*, 154
as *philia*, 149, 155
elements of, 154, 155
Tillich on, 154
Luhmann, Niklas, 114
Luther, Martin, 106, 109
MacIntyre, Alasdair, 36, 83
Madsen, Richard, 11
magic, 52, 71, 127
Makuta, Eddy Lundemba, 70
Mammon, 36, 51, 52, 53, 84, 85
managerial competence, 140
Marx, Karl, 23, 24
material forces, 120, 121
meaning, 24, 37, 51, 53–54, 55–59, 63–64, 108, 111
Meditations, 29
Messiah, 60. See also Jesus Christ
methodological individualism, 28
Miletus, 115
Minerva Owl, 135
miracle, 71, 72, 73, 137
modes of life, 127, 128, 140
    coercive, 127, 128, 140
    gift, 128, 140
    market, 127
    sales, 127, 140
monads, 95, 97
monasteries, 116
monetary economics, 8, 26, 96
monetary policy
    and integration, 155
    and justice, 9–10, 28–30, 150
    and stimulation, 155
    and the promotion of sociality, 155–156
    and transformation, 155
    and work, 9–10, 138, 149–156
    definition, 9, 138, 150–153
    ethics of, 9, 10–13, 28
    significance of, xix, 54, 156
money creation, 11, 75
money supply, 9, 11, 26, 73, 151
    and work, 9–10, 138, 149–156
money,
    and credit-money, 144, 145
    and debt, 25–26, 142–148
    and earmarking, 23, 24, 51
    and environmental pollution, 25–30
    and personhood, 94–97
    as dead identity, 74
    as dead matter, 74
    as *relational thing*, 62
    as seen by accountants, 22
    as social relations, 24–25, 51, 61–63, 142–148
    as two-edged sword, 154
    defined, 22–25
    god among commodities, 24
    metallic, 145
    ontology of, 137
    state theory of, 144
monks, 116
    Cistercian, 116
moral bookkeeping, 139. See also ethical scorekeeping
morality community, 107
Moses, 102
Mosques, 31, 36
multiple, 136
multiplicity, 136–137
mutuality, 9, 10, 54, 62, 73, 97, 126, 138, 151, 155–156

N

Nancy, Jean-Luc, 126
natality, 60, 137
nature, 28–30
Nelson, Benjamin, 119
Nelson, Robert, 104n7
neoclassical economics, 28, 94–95
New Being, 59–61, 64
New, the, 59, 61–62
Nicholas of Cusa, 120
Niebuhr, Richard, xv, 36
Nietzsche, Friedrich, 120, 130, 131
non-asset, 133
nonbeing, 154
not-asset, 133
Nussbaum, Martha, 71, 132, 133

Subject Index

O

obligation, 129, 130, 131, 132
Odysseus, 84
offerings, 7, 19, 45, 67, 82
offsite, 83
Olive presses, 115
Olivi, Pierre de Jean, 106
ontology of numbers, 36
Oord, Thomas Jay, 148
opportunism, 107
option, 115
organizational spirit of leadership, 73
original sin, 84
Orpheus, 85

P

Paccioli, Luca, 119
Parable of the talents, 114
paradox, 1, 37
parallax, 1
parousia, 126
Pascal wager, 117
Pascal, Blaise, 106, 117
passive reading, 124
pathos, 153
Patočka, Jan, 2n2
perception, 29, 108, 110, 116, 121
perichorectic sociality, 62
personal liabilities, 87–89
personhood, xvi, xviii, 54, 94–97, 126
    ontology of, 93, 94
    relational, xviii, 97
physical laws, 115
Piper, Otto A., 95
Pixley, Jocelyn, 147, 148
Plato, 152
Polemos, 29
polis, 61
politics 53, 58–59, 93–94
pollution. See environmental pollution
poor, 10, 27, 70–73, 118, 138, 149, 152, 153
Pope John Paul, 108
Pope Leo XII, 108

potentiality, 51, 137, 138
praxis, 56, 58, 122, 149, 154
    of justice, 149
premium, 110, 118
Price, Richard, 117
Princess Medea, 85
Probability, 110, 115, 117
profanation, 92
property rights, 101–102, 109
prophets, 138
proton, 65
providence, 104, 105, 116, 120
Puritans, 103

Q

Quakers, 107

R

rational universe, 115
ratios, 7–8, 47–50
    current, 47, 49
    debt to asset, 48
    defensive, 50
    liquidity, 47, 49
    total debt to net assets, 49
real presence, 124
real, the, 58, 59, 60
reality itself, 134
reciprocity, 29, 127, 131, 156
redemption, 1, 16, 60, 92
Reformation, 103
Relationship-Product Format, 6
religare, 91–92
religio, 91–92
Rerum Novarum, 108
revealed preferences, 107
Rice, Michael, 129–130
risk analysis, 47
risk management, 115–117, 119
ritual of struggles, 11
rituals, xv, 8, 9, 9–11, 52
Roman Catholic Church, 102, 108
Romans, 110
Rousseau, Jacques, 28

Subject Index

S

sacerdotal functions, 33–34, 35
Sacks, Jonathan, 103
sacred oath, xviii, 92
Samuel, 102
Samuelson, Paul, 23
Sandel, Michael, 93
Sanneh, Lamin, 141
Saravia, Louis, 106
savings rate, 111
scales of justice, 93
Schulde, 130
Schumpeter, Joseph, 118
semantic reading, 135
semiotic triangle, 113
Shubik, Martin, 119
Simmel, Georg, 23, 145, 146
Sirens, 84–85
situation, 136–137
Smith, Adam, 104–106
social justice, xv, xix, xx, 5, 9, 150
Social Security, 34–35
social trinitarianism, 63
spheres of life, 50–52
spheres of life and spiritual energies, 50–53
    dominion (religion), 52, 53
    eros, 52, 53
    mammon, 52, 53
    mars, 52, 53
    muses, 52, 53
Stackhouse, Max, 51, 52, 118, 121
Stark, Rodney, 101
statistical inference, 117
stewardship leadership, xii
stock of money, 73
Summa de arithmetic, geometria et proportionalita, 119
Sutcliffe, Bob, 27
Symposium, 152
Synagogues, 31, 36
synergies, 127

T

T-Account, 40–41
Tanner, Kathryn, 95n11
taxes,
    housing allowance, 35
    Medicare taxes, 34
    self-employment tax, 34, 35
techne, 53, 122
technocratic management, 58
telos, 56, 93, 153
temple, 9, 11, 36
tertium quid, 64
Thales of Melitus, 115
the said, 124
theological framework, 53–55
theology-in-motion, xiii, xv, xix, 9, 25, 35, 50, 74, 83, 94
theonomously, 65
Theory of Moral Sentiments, 105
Tillich, Paul, 59–60, 96, 136n24, 154
time, 7, 57, 60, 108, 109, 110–113
    attitudes toward, 108, 109, 110–113
    preference rate, 111
    preference rate and justice, 112
    selling of, 118
transaction costs, 107
translation, 1, 141
transparency, see chapter 6
    and evaluation, 76, 78
    standards of, 77–82
Treasury Department, 26, 143
Trial Balance, 39, 40–42, 126
Trinity, 54, 63, 98, 148, 149. See also Godhead
trust, 52, 77, 79, 81, 87, 101, 102, 106–107, 109, 116, 142, 145, 147
    production of, 101, 106

U

ultimate concern, 131, 135
uncertainty, 113, 115, 117
unfreedoms, 152
unity-in-difference, xii, 64, 148
universal code, 123

Subject Index

usury, 112,118, 119
utility, 29, 105, 112

V

valuation, 29, 88, 106, 111, 120
Venice, 144
virtues, 36, 83–84, 94, 108
vita activa, 109
vita contemplative, 109
void, 136–137
volatility, 47
Volf, Miroslav, 109, 127–128, 140

W

Wall Street. Xiv, 108, 109, 113, 119
Walmart, 129–130
Waterman, Anthony, 105
Wealth of Nations, 104
Weber, Max, 23, 62, 107, 108, 109, 120, 146n8
Wennerlind, Carl, 143
Wolf, Martin, 10
work ethic, 101, 107, 108–109
work, definition of, 9–10, 138, 150
work, theology of, 149–156

Y

Yeats, William Butler, 12

Z

Zelizer, Viviana, 24, 25, 50, 116
zero, 119, 133, 136–138
zero-sum game, 114, 126
Žižek, Slavoj, 133

www.ingramcontent.com/pod-product-compliance
Lightning Source LLC
Chambersburg PA
CBHW071449150426
43191CB00008B/1289